THE TRADITION OF LIBERAL THEOLOGY

The Tradition of Liberal Theology

Michael J. Langford

WILLIAM B. EERDMANS PUBLISHING COMPANY

GRAND RAPIDS, MICHIGAN / CAMBRIDGE, U.K.

Published 2014 by
Wm. B. Eerdmans Publishing Co.
2140 Oak Industrial Drive N.E., Grand Rapids, Michigan 49505 /
P.O. Box 163, Cambridge CB3 9PU U.K.

Printed in the United States of America

20 19 18 17 16 15 14   7 6 5 4 3 2 1

Library of Congress Cataloging-in-Publication Data

Langford, Michael J., 1931-
The tradition of liberal theology / Michael J. Langford.
        pages   cm
Includes bibliographical references and index.
ISBN 978-0-8028-6981-4 (pbk.: alk. paper)
1. Liberalism (Religion) — History.
2. Church history.   I. Title.

BR1615.L365   2013
230'.046 — dc23
                                2013030579

www.eerdmans.com

Contents

———∞∞∞———

CONTENTS

Preface

What is commonly referred to as the "liberal tradition" in Christian thinking has a long history, one that goes back at least as far as Origen, who was writing in the third century of the Christian era. This tradition, so I claim, should be understood as a variation on what I call "mainstream" Christianity, that is, one that accepts the statements of the Apostles' Creed, albeit with a certain latitude in the interpretation of some clauses. It is thus to be contrasted with certain later theological positions, sometimes also called "liberal," that depart from the kind of faith position supported by Origen and a whole range of followers, including Richard Hooker and William Chillingworth. Because of this strong connection with the core statements of the Creed, I think that the tradition I describe can properly be referred to as "liberal orthodoxy" — though, unfortunately, this term has also been used in different ways.

Needless to say, the tradition that I am investigating here was not called liberal until that term acquired something of its present meaning — according to the Oxford English Dictionary — in about 1780. In the first chapter I provide an initial account of the nature of the tradition and defend the use of the word "liberal" in order to describe it. Thereafter, I seek to explore the essential nature of the tradition in three ways. In the second chapter I describe eleven typical characteristics of the tradition. (In doing so, I respectfully cite Wittgenstein's claim that many concepts are better described in terms of a set of typical characteristics than by finding a single "defining" characteristic.) In the third chapter I provide vignettes of thirteen representatives of liberal theology, or, in some cases, of certain aspects of it. The fourth chapter contrasts the tradition with some of the more widely held alternatives, namely, more conservative forms of Christian belief, secular humanism, and non-Christian religions. For the most part, I am concerned with the nature and history of liberal theology up to about 1900; however, I also refer to issues that have emerged since that time and to some of the philosophers and theologians who have responded to them. I believe that it will also become evident why I believe that the tradition is of prime importance for the world of today. What I call the liberal tradition in Christianity has interesting parallels in most other major religions, but, apart from occasional references, I do not describe them in this book. However, it is encouraging to note how often those in different liberal traditions speak with a common voice.

Throughout this book I have tried to write at a level that is somewhere between what one finds in most books of academic philosophy or theology, which are frequently too technical for the ordinary intelligent reader, and what one finds in most popular books, which often do not sufficiently challenge the mind. In other words, this book attempts to build a bridge between the academic and the popular.

This volume is a sequel to two other books I have written in the area of liberal theology, the more academic *A Liberal Theology for the Twenty-First Century* (Aldershot, UK: Ashgate, 2001) and the more popularly written *Unblind Faith* (1st ed., London: SCM Press, 1982; 2nd, expanded ed., Tunbridge Wells, UK: Parapress, 2010). This new book contains a number of themes found in those earlier books, and in some passages (as in the discussion of the Anglican divine Jeremy Taylor and of the topics of original sin, redemption, and alternative lifestyles) I have adapted material from the second edition of *Unblind Faith*.

Since the two books referred to above have attempted to give a systematic account of the principal theological doctrines of Christianity from within a liberal perspective, I do not try to provide such an account in the present volume (though there is a brief discussion of the doctrine of the Trinity in chapter 4). However, in many places the implications of a liberal approach for such doctrines are evident.

viii

CHAPTER ONE

The Meaning of the Term "Liberal Theology"

———— ❧ ————

This chapter begins to explore what the term "liberal theology" means in the context of Christian theology. I shall argue that it refers to a recognizable tradition in which there is a balance between religious faith and human rationality. This tradition is closely associated with the notion of "apologetics" and thus with a presentation of Christianity that appeals to reason rather than to emotion. According to this tradition, it does not follow that emotion should never be appealed to — for example, in sermons — but that there is *also* the need for a reasoned defense of the faith.

For many contemporary people, the term "apologetics" is as unclear as the term "liberal theology," suggesting, perhaps, that one is "apologizing" for a position in a way that parallels how one might apologize for a mistake. Traditionally, however, apologetics meant a robust *defense,* and in my view an apologetics of this kind is particularly appropriate today, when there is the assumption among so many contemporaries that a truly rational person will have little or no time for religious beliefs. As a professional philosopher, I am appalled at how often I find this assumption, often combined with accounts of traditional religious positions that are quite simply caricatures of religion — at least of religion at its best.[1] The position that I

---

1. In many intellectual circles this view has been around for much longer than is often realized. For example, in the preface (strictly speaking, the "Advertisement") to his

shall support in this book is that, far from religion being irrational, at least some forms of religious belief (what I identify with the term "the tradition of liberal theology") are more rational than those of many contemporary atheists. Among many atheists there is a kind of mantra that goes: "Science is based on reason, religion is based on authority and dogma" — with a number of variants that amount to the same claim. This mantra is misleading even with regard to science, because it does not capture the deep, perhaps existential, commitment to truth that typifies the scientific enterprise; yet it is particularly unfair with regard to religion.

There are certainly forms of religion that are based purely on authority and dogma. In chapter 3, for example, we shall see how the Cambridge Platonists characterized such forms of religion as "superstition." However, there is a fundamental *rational* principle that we should judge sincerely held positions by their best examples, and not by their perversions. Just as it would be absurd to judge atheism by the likes of Stalin, so it is absurd to judge all religion by the likes of its fundamentalist followers. In this book I shall explore a version of Christianity that chooses rationality over authority, and that only uses the word "dogma," if at all, for what are held to be important teachings that are the result of deep reflection.

My point here could easily be misunderstood. In the context of an account of what rationality can be taken to mean, as provided in chapter 2 (under the subheading "Reason and Revelation in Harmony"), I argue that rational people can be theists or atheists or agnostics. (I also hold that it is possible for rational people to be monists,[2] or logical posi-

---

The Analogy of Religion, written in 1736 (ed. W. E. Gladstone [London: Oxford University Press, 1907]), Bishop Joseph Butler notes how often it is taken for granted that Christianity has been discovered to be "fictitious."

2. Monism means literally "one principle," or simply "oneness," and is usually contrasted with dualism, meaning "two principles," and pluralism, meaning "many principles." Monistic systems of philosophy, such as that of Advaita Hinduism, deny that there is any real separation between the supreme principle of the universe (whether or not this is called "God") and everything else. By contrast, in classical theism God is the Creator who created the universe by a voluntary act; therefore, a kind of dualism is involved — i.e., a radical distinction between Creator and creature. (In other contexts "dualism" usually refers to a different distinction, namely, that between mind and body.) Some twentieth-century Christians, most notably A. N. Whitehead and Charles Hartshorne, introduced an alternative form of theism, sometimes called "panen-

tivists, though perhaps not in accordance with the rather crude way in which this philosophy was formulated in the 1930s.[3] It is also possible, I hold, for a rational person to follow some non-Christian versions of theism, particularly those that have an equivalent to the liberal theology that I describe. (But these are not the focus of this book.) However, many people hold fundamentally irrational versions of all these positions because they have never properly evaluated the traditions they reject — and sometimes the ones they adopt — and understand them not as they are at their best but as they are represented by some kind of caricature. For example, my most fundamental disagreement with Richard Dawkins does not concern his atheism as such (a position that, as I have just indicated, I believe can be held by a rational person); but it concerns his consistent caricature of the best version of the position he attacks. He does not consider what Terry Eagleton calls "the toughest case."[4]

It will be obvious to those familiar with current debates in the philosophy of religion that my emphasis on the rationality of at least one form of Christian faith is sharply opposed not only to the views of many atheists and agnostics but also to the views of some Christians. Probably the most challenging form of a Christian rejection of the approach followed in this book is to be found in the movement known as "dialectical theology" associated with Karl Barth (1886-1968). In chapter 4, when I review certain alternatives to liberal theology, I shall summarize the difference between my approach and Barth's — and the reasons for it.

Prior to any defense of liberal theology, either in the context of opposition from fellow Christians — such as Barthians — or from non-Christians, there is a need to describe the nature and history of this tradition, and this will be the principal task of this book. The focus will be on the nature of this tradition up to about 1900, but I shall make some reference to liberal theology in its more recent formulations, especially near the end of chapter 3 (in the section entitled "Twentieth-century Themes").

---

theism," which suggests a less radical and less dualistic distinction between God and creation.

3. I shall expand on the meaning of logical positivism in the section on materialism in chapter 4.

4. Terry Eagleton, "Lunging, Flailing, Mispunching," *The London Review of Books,* October 19, 2006, pp. 32-34.

Unfortunately, the word "liberal," both with respect to theology and in other contexts, has become ambiguous and is often used merely as a term of abuse. An example is when people refer to "woolly liberals": in such instances it is unclear whether there can be non-woolly liberals or whether the word "liberal" is a catch term for those whose moderate opinions they dislike. In the context of defending a rational approach to theology, I considered dropping the term "liberal"; but I have decided instead to defend it on the grounds that, properly understood, it stands — within Christianity and many other major religions — for traditions that deserve a better press and a better appreciation. Furthermore, other terms that one could suggest present similar problems of misunderstanding. For example, liberal Christianity should not be confused with many *radical* forms of so-called Christian belief that deny the reality of God and other central Christian teachings. In particular, "nonrealist" accounts of God, supported by some significant theologians, including Don Cupitt, do not represent the liberal tradition described in this book.[5] As Dorothy Emmet once wrote, "Religion loses its nerve when it ceases to believe that it expresses in some way truth about our relation to a reality beyond ourselves which ultimately concerns us."[6]

One common misunderstanding of liberal theology arises from connecting it too closely to the similar term "liberalism." In 1879, John Henry Newman wrote: "Liberalism in religion is the doctrine that there is no positive truth in religion, but that one creed is as good as another. . . ."[7] Newman's dislike of certain forms of liberalism that he encountered is understandable; but if his statement is taken to characterize liberal theology, either as presented here or as it has been used by many other writers, it will be seen to be completely unfair. For example, not only do typical liberals hold that there are crucial "truths" in religion (though those may not include all the ones accepted by Cardinal Newman), they are

---

5. For these writers, "God" is a word that may usefully be used to refer to an ideal or a myth, but not an actually existing reality.

6. Dorothy Emmet, *The Nature of Metaphysical Thinking* (London: Macmillan, 1966), p. 4.

7. Quoted in Alec R. Vidler, *Essays in Liberality* (London: SCM Press, 1957), p. 10. In *The Idea of a University* (1852), Newman uses the word "liberal" (in "liberal education") with positive force.

usually equally insistent on some "absolutes," or matters of intrinsic good and evil in the area of ethics.[8] The difference from the point of view espoused by Newman is that some of the things liberals regard as intrinsically wrong are not the same as those held to be so by conservative theologians, especially in the past. For both the churchmen behind the Inquisition and for John Calvin, it was intrinsically wrong to allow heretics to live, while for liberals, killing them — especially by burning them alive — is and always has been intrinsically evil. More positively, both conservative and liberal Christians (along with many secular thinkers) believe in the "intrinsic" worth of each individual person and accept some version of Kant's moral principle that all persons should be treated as ends in themselves — not merely as means.

If we concentrate on what liberal theology is, rather than on what it is not, we can get a sense of what the term stands for from examples of those who have either upheld the tradition through their lives and writings or who have contributed to it in significant ways. In chapter 3, I shall provide vignettes of thirteen of these key men and women. In these people we shall find a profound respect for Christian Scripture coupled with a growing realization that the inspiration of the Bible does not need to be seen as verbal and literal. In addition, in the majority of cases we find that all the fundamental Christian doctrines found in the Apostles' Creed are affirmed. In no significant sense were these people "woolly liberals"; rather, with the exception of Hannah Barnard, they represent one version of what I call mainstream Christianity. By "mainstream" I do not mean the same thing as when I say "liberal"; rather, I refer to the wider class of those

8. Not all liberals like to refer to "absolutes" with regard to ethics because of the different ways in which the term is used. In my view, there are absolutes in ethics, but these are not absolute rules (such as "never tell a lie") but absolute principles, which — unlike rules — do not tell one exactly what to do. For example, "always seek to be honest" is a principle that one should always try to uphold; but it does not tell one exactly what to do when it conflicts with another moral principle, such as "seek to protect the lives of the innocent." Genuine ethical dilemmas arise when such principles are in tension, and then a judgment has to be made that is not simply a matter of following some higher rule. Moral principles like these are absolute in the sense that they always carry weight, and they can only be set aside because of tension with another moral principle, not for our convenience. See R. M. Dworkin, "Is Law a System of Rules," reprinted in R. M. Dworkin, ed., *The Philosophy of Law* (Oxford: Oxford University Press, 1977).

who, unlike the ones I call "radicals," uphold all or nearly all the traditional doctrines associated with Christianity. Mainstream Christianity, given this usage, can then be divided into more conservative and more liberal traditions. The latter group is the subject of this book. Consequently, the tradition I am describing could be termed "liberal orthodoxy," and should not be identified with the somewhat loose way in which the word "liberal" is frequently used in the context of theology.[9] John Habgood, who describes himself as a "conservative liberal" in his *Confessions of a Conservative Liberal* (1988), would certainly count as an exemplar of the tradition I describe.

Because I see the tradition with which I am concerned as a variant on what I call mainstream Christianity (of which all forms accept the essential teaching of the Apostles' Creed), there are some differences of emphasis from Gary Dorrien's in his three-volume *The Making of American Liberal Theology*, which covers the period 1805 to 2005.[10] First, Dorrien marks the beginning of what he calls "liberal theology" within the eighteenth century, whereas I see it as a continuation of a much older tradition. Second, a central characteristic of the tradition with which Dorrien is concerned is a rejection of "external authority."[11] In my analysis, suspicion of the authority of either church or political leaders is a genuine feature of the liberal tradition, one of several "typical characteristics." However, it can too easily imply that a reasoned approach to religion must be in ten-

9. *Liberal Orthodoxy,* by Henry W. Clark (London: Chapman and Hall, 1914), is the title of an interesting book published early in the twentieth century. Clark sees the early nineteenth century as the beginnings of what he calls "liberal orthodoxy," though he refers to the Cambridge Platonists as "forerunners" of the tradition. He places the origins in Germany, especially with Schleiermacher, and a little later in England, with "the early Oriel school," which was promoted by Richard Whateley, Renn Hampden, Matthew Arnold, and others. Clark's basic definition of the tradition is in terms of "the effort to marry . . . Christian faith to progressive thought" (p. 1), which has similarities to my own account, especially when he relates the tradition to the rejection of the verbal inspiration of Scripture (p. 15n).

10. Gary Dorrien, *The Making of American Liberal Theology:* vol. 1, *Imagining Progressive Religion, 1805-1900* (Louisville: Westminster John Knox Press, 2001); vol. 2, *Idealism, Realism, and Modernity, 1900-1950* (Louisville: Westminster John Knox Press, 2003); vol. 3, *Crisis, Irony, and Postmodernity, 1950-2005* (Louisville: Westminster John Knox Press, 2006).

11. Dorrien, *The Making of American Liberal Theology,* 1:xxiii.

sion with one kind of external authority, namely, that of what is believed to be revelation. Dorrien's liberal theology makes place for scriptural authority, but not to "settle or establish truth claims about matters of fact." However, this leaves unclear what kind of relevance the Bible has for the historical life of Jesus in general and the resurrection in particular. Third, Dorrien's definition of the tradition leads him to include within it Unitarianism and other — what I would call more "radical" — reformulations of Christianity, which, notwithstanding my respect for some of them, are not part of what I identify as the tradition that runs from before Origen to the likes of Joseph Lightfoot. (In this connection, Dorrien usefully distinguishes two kinds of Unitarianism, one of which is a kind of "Harvard style," accepting a miracle-working God, and another rooted in an Emersonian spiritualism.)[12]

I have already indicated my belief that it is possible to hold rational forms of both theism and atheism. What needs to be added is that the word "theism" is used in several ways. The kind of theism generally supported in what I identify as the liberal tradition can be called "classical theism," which includes both the idea of a Creator ex nihilo and of a God who is in relationship with individual persons. In the case of Paul Tillich (who identifies God with what is of "Ultimate Concern") and several of the other theologians discussed by Dorrien, it is sometimes hard to decide whether to class them as "classical theists" or as theists of some other kind, or in some cases — though not in the case of Tillich — as atheists. At the same time, Dorrien's emphasis on the liberal tradition as one of mediation has much in common with my approach, even though he includes Schleiermacher as a typical exemplar and I do not, for reasons that will emerge later in this chapter. The mediation with which I am chiefly concerned, following Hooker, is that between conservative forms of Catholicism and Calvinism, whereas Dorrien's is between a literalist Christianity, which emphasized the substitutionary sacrifice of Christ, and the atheism of French-style revolutionaries.

However, my somewhat different approach to what should count as liberal theology does not diminish my respect for Dorrien's scholarly work, which brings before us the writings of many important and some-

12. Dorrien, *The Making of American Liberal Theology*, 2:1; 1:68.

times neglected theologians, such as Horace Bushnell. The main differences are that he surveys a much narrower range of the tradition in terms of both place and time and a broader range of what should be included within the tradition.

Returning to the attempt to describe the typical characteristics of the tradition on which I am focusing, we should underscore the importance of those nineteenth-century Christians who, from the first publication of Darwin's *Origin of Species* (in 1859) found no need to see an opposition between biblical truth and scientific truth, including the theory of evolution. Examples include the Anglican clergymen Frederick Temple and Charles Kingsley and the American scientist Asa Gray, Darwin's friend.

Yet another pointer to what liberal theology has meant is found in the life and teaching of J. F. D. Maurice and the development of it by his followers. Not only was Maurice fired from his professorship in London for teaching that hellfire was not an eternal place of punishment (in 1853); he was also one of the principal founders of Christian socialism.[13] This was an attempt to see how the social implications of the Bible raised fundamental political questions. The insight that there is a connection between the gospel and social justice was not, of course, first made by Maurice. One need only recall the antislavery movement of the eighteenth century (spearheaded first by Quakers such as John Woolman and later by a number of Anglicans and Methodists). However, with Maurice we see a new concentration on the need to reorder the whole social order. This demanded an intellectual understanding of the gospel that could provide — and that still provides — an alternative to Marxism for those whose fundamental concern is social justice. It is for this reason that there are interconnections between the use of "liberal" in theology and its use in political philosophy. Within politics the term has suffered from the same kind of ambiguity as has the usage of the term in theology. However, while we should be aware of the interconnections, liberalism in politics is not the subject of this book.

---

13. This term has been given several rather different meanings; for Maurice, the emphasis was more on the requirement of justice to provide for the underprivileged than on any system of state ownership.

Nevertheless, the relationship of the liberal traditions in theology and in politics is of such importance — and the likely source of so much misunderstanding — that a further comment is in order. Both movements were strongly influenced by the Enlightenment, but this does not mean, in either case, that the main themes of the Enlightenment should be taken onboard uncritically. In the case of what is popularly called "political liberalism," there are, as in "theological liberalism," a number of typical characteristics that have much in common with Enlightenment thinking. Some of these, I suggest, should be wholeheartedly supported by the theological liberal, for example, the separation of religious law from civil law; the separation of powers (executive, legislative, and judicial); toleration of beliefs that do not directly incite violence; the legal support of basic human rights, and so on. Other Enlightenment ideas should be seriously questioned, for example, the idea that religion is a purely private matter that has no major implications for politics; the claim that a secular philosophy can give an adequate account of what human happiness and fulfillment consist in; and the denial that the church is a global community that should have a voice in political debate.

The Oxford English Dictionary defines the relevant sense of the word "liberal" as "free from narrow prejudice; open-minded, candid," and it quotes Edward Gibbon, in 1781, as the first-known reference to this usage. However, as I have indicated in my reference to Dorrien's work, I must emphasize that what I am calling the "liberal tradition" in theology arose long before the term was applied to it. Immediately prior to Gibbon's use of the word, the tradition tended to be called "latitudinarian," and other earlier terms had a similar, though not identical sense, including Arminian (because of Arminius's emphasis on free will) and, occasionally, Alexandrine (because of the huge influence of Clement and Origen, both of whom taught in Alexandria). The nature of this tradition will become clearer in the next chapter, where we will consider eleven of its key characteristics. There is considerable overlap with "modernism," for example, within a movement given that name in late nineteenth- and early twentieth-century Roman Catholicism, whose followers sometimes referred to themselves as "liberal Catholics."[14] On occasion, the

---

14. See, e.g., A. Leslie Lilley, ed., *What We Want — An Open Letter to Pius X from a*

term "modernism" has also been used within Protestantism to indicate an antifundamentalist movement that has much in common with the liberal tradition, especially in the 1920s, following an influential sermon preached by Harry Emerson Fosdick (at a Presbyterian church in New York City), entitled "Shall the Fundamentalists Win?"[15] Nevertheless, I have decided not to use the term "modernism" largely because it suggests too much in the way of innovation, whereas the tradition I am describing tends to see itself as rooted in the priorities of the first Christians. There is also some overlap with the "Broad Church" in England and the "Moderates" in Scotland, but these terms suggest a vagueness in doctrine that is not typical of the tradition I am concerned with.

Although I want to emphasize the continuity of contemporary liberal theology with an ancient tradition, I also want to admit that it has gathered some features that are genuinely new. This is not surprising if one believes that theology should be undertaken afresh in every generation so that it can respond to the thinking of the time. One example of change is in the attitude toward the way in which faith is to be considered a virtue, and I want to comment on this matter.

In a thoughtful article in which he reviews *The Dawkins Delusion?* by Alister and Joanna McGrath, the philosopher Anthony Kenny argues that, despite the many errors in Richard Dawkins's *The God Delusion* (to which the McGrath book is a response), Dawkins's account of faith "is closer to traditional Christianity than McGrath's."[16] Faith (within traditional Christianity) is irrevocable, and "a faith that is held tentatively is no true faith." Unlike Dawkins, Kenny does not deny that there can be good arguments to support faith; but such arguments cannot have anything like the degree of cogency that would rationally justify irrevocable commitment. For this reason, faith should not be regarded as a virtue.

Group of Priests (London: John Murray, 1907), p. xix. The priests argue that the "old coercive methods must be abandoned or relaxed," and they defend "a more liberal consideration towards the religious activities of the laity" (p. 25).

15. See Ernestine van der Wall, *The Enemy Within: Religion, Science, and Modernism* (Uhlenbeck Lecture, Netherlands Institute for Advanced Study, 2007). Some of the different forms of "modernism" are discussed in Gary Dorrien, *The Making of American Liberal Theology*, esp. 2:10-20.

16. *The Times Literary Supplement*, August 17, 2007, pp. 26-27.

I disagree with Kenny here because, even in traditional Christianity, I think that *part* of what faith has meant has been the courage to stand by one's sincere commitments even in the face of death, and this courage can be genuinely virtuous. However, Kenny makes a good case for questioning the virtuous character of the kind of faith so often lauded in the Christian tradition. Although faith has been classed as one of the theological virtues, if it is described in the way that Kenny claims, it is not a virtue. (Further, if it is seen as a gift of grace, it might be one of what Aristotle calls the "natural virtues," but not a true virtue, or *hexis,* which has to be acquired within a process that involves some internal effort.[17])

However, I think it is still possible to describe faith as a virtue, apart from the component of courage, if we have the kind of nuanced approach to the rationality of belief that the liberal tradition seeks to bring about. Many Christian writers of the last century have taken a very different approach to doubt than most previous ones. Doubt, for a liberal thinker, is no longer regarded as a sin, but rather as a genuine part of intellectual inquiry in matters of faith.[18] (In chapter 3, I shall note a similar emphasis, even in the 1500s, both in Sebastian Castellio's book *The Art of Doubting* and in Richard Hooker's rejection of "certainty of evidence" regarding matters of faith.) The opposite of faith is not doubt but faithlessness, or the lack of serious commitment to what one has come to believe. Here there is a shift in the meaning of faith away from irrevocable belief and toward commitment, but not a blind commitment; rather, it is a willingness to live in accordance with the beliefs one has come to hold — in many cases, by a long process of reflection. *Pistis* (the New Testament word that has been translated as "faith") usually refers to this kind of commitment rather than to belief as such.

17. Aristotle, *Nichomachean Ethics,* trans. H. Rackham, Loeb series (London: Heinemann, 1926), XI, 13, 1144b. A "natural virtue" is a *phusike arete.*

18. The late Archbishop Anthony Bloom would not generally be called a "liberal" (though he had many liberal views), but he had revealing things to say about the positive role that doubt can play. See Bloom, *God and Man* (London: Darton, Longman and Todd, 1971), p. 38. For an interesting analysis of different kinds of doubt, see M. Polanyi, *Personal Knowledge* (London: Routledge, 1958), chap. 9. Descartes, as is well known, advocated a kind of systematic doubt in order to uncover a sure foundation for philosophy, but he did not advocate doubt concerning the existence of God once he had (to his satisfaction) proved his existence.

The term "irrevocability" is the crucial one here. Kenny may accurately describe how many (though not all) Christians in the past have regarded faith, but "irrevocability" strikes the wrong note for the kind of commitment that many Christians advocate. For example, we should try to approach an argument with an intelligent opponent with a genuine openness. Partly because I have been a Christian for many years, I do indeed have a fairly high level of conviction that many of my beliefs are both true and defensible by rational argument (though this does not mean that they are "provable"). However, not only do I accept that I may have many new things to learn (for example, from a scholarly Buddhist), but also that, in principle, I could be wrong in some of my most fundamental beliefs. Sticking to them, regardless of the argument, would be a vice rather than a virtue, though it would be reasonable to spend a considerable time in further discussion and reflection rather than abandon them in the middle of a single discussion.

There is more. The kind of conviction that intelligent people develop with respect to not only religious matters, but also to ethical, political, and perhaps aesthetic matters, involves more than pure ratiocination. This is one of the places where it is very hard to draw sharp lines between logic and other — more emotional — aspects of the human psyche (a theme that I will revisit in the section entitled "Reason and Revelation in Harmony" in chapter 2 and in the section on John Smith in chapter 3). For example, the commitment of many secular humanists to the fight for human rights and against torture (which I share) is much more than a matter of logic; but it is not therefore "irrational." If this kind of commitment can be virtuous, then perhaps so can certain kinds of faith. Indeed, certain moral convictions, regardless of religious belief, may represent a special class of a "faith position."

A realization of the importance of the nonrational (which is not to be confused with the "irrational," wherein there is manifest prejudice or inconsistency or bad argument) leads to an appreciation of the limits of any "apology" on behalf of Christianity. For many people, a need to "belong" takes precedence over what they believe, and this implies that for most followers of a religion, the heart of their faith is far more a matter of shared activities than of particular beliefs. Roger Scruton has written of the two distinct strands "that compose religious consciousness," that of belief and that of membership, the latter meaning "all the customs, ceremonies and practices whereby the sacred is renewed." He goes on to warn of an inappropriate emphasis on what is believed rather than on the practices that bind people together.[19]

This need to find a balance between the rational and the nonrational within any adequate account of what religion is about can be further explored via a reflection on the importance of Friedrich Schleiermacher for the theme of this essay. Schleiermacher is often referred to as the father of the Protestant version of liberal theology, and in the light of this it may seem surprising that in chapter 3 he is not included in the list of significant exemplars (even though my list does not pretend to be in any way exhaustive). In my view, there are several reasons why he is not a typical exemplar of what I call "the liberal tradition," and an examination of these reasons will help to explain what I hold the nature of this tradition to be.

First — and most important — Schleiermacher's emphasis on feeling is too much in tension with the generally rational nature of the tradition I describe. I need to express this point carefully. The most common word that Schleiermacher uses (usually translated in English as "feeling") is *Gefühl*. In many contexts, "feeling" is the most natural translation; but the word can also connote "instinct" or "intuitive grasp." This is even more evident in his use of the word *Anschauung*, a word he often used in earlier editions of his major works but subsequently dropped, probably because he wanted to dissociate his position from the ethical idealism of contemporaneous philosophers such as Fichte. *Anschauung* carries something of the notion of perception or intuition; in religious feeling, with which Schleiermacher is primarily concerned, it is a kind of immediate self-consciousness, or even a *discernment* of a divine presence. He is not opposed to the use of reason, but the foundation of his philosophy of religion is an "immediate feeling of absolute dependence" on God.[20]

---

19. Roger Scruton, "The Philosophy of Wine," in Barry C. Smith, ed., *Matters of Taste: The Philosophy of Wine* (Oxford: Signal Books, 2007), p. 17.

20. F. Schleiermacher, *The Christian Faith* (Edinburgh: T&T Clark, 1928; English trans. of 2nd German ed.), para. 32. Hereafter, specific paragraph references to this work appear in parentheses in the text.

In due course I shall note that some people whom I present as typical exemplars of the liberal tradition, in particular the Cambridge Platonist John Smith, are aware that one cannot always drive a hard line between the thinking and emotional responses of a person. Nevertheless, there is still a contrast between Schleiermacher's position and that of the typical form of rationalism found within what I identify as the liberal tradition, which includes an attempt, from the time of the early apologists and of Origen, to marry the best of Greek philosophy with the heart of Hebrew piety. Reason, for Schleiermacher, is a kind of historical phenomenon, working in the context of a particular person and a particular history; it is never something universal, as it is in at least some Greek thinkers. Second, Schleiermacher's acceptance of the core doctrines of the Apostles' Creed is different in emphasis from that of typical liberals within the tradition. Although there is a certain latitude in the interpretation of creedal statements within the tradition (such as whether or not to take literally the virginity of Mary or the descent into hell), and although there is sometimes a fuzzy line between liberal and conservative theologians (as will become clear), Schleiermacher's account of the central Christian doctrines reads more like an approval of one way of interpreting the overall religious experience of man than that of seeing fundamental truths within the Christian religion. He writes: "Christian doctrines are accounts of the Christian religious affections set forth in speech" (para. 15). This approach is especially evident in his account of the Trinity (paras. 170-72). In Henry Clark's words, Schleiermacher "sat loosely to some of the articles of the customary creeds"; and while he considered himself a Trinitarian, he doubted creedal language "as given in the usual formulae."[21]

A third reason, closely related to the second, is that Schleiermacher shows little concern for defending Christian teaching over against that of other faiths. His references to Judaism and Islam, for example, suggest that he sees them as positive attempts to respond to the same awareness of the divine presence in the context of other seminal figures in the history of religion.

Nevertheless, Schleiermacher had a strong influence on liberal ex-

21. Henry W. Clark, *Liberal Orthodoxy*, pp. 107-8.

ponents of Christianity, largely because of his response to the Enlightenment. He did not follow the reaction to the Enlightenment that tried to defend the faith primarily in terms of providing a moral agenda for humanity, nor the reaction that tried to go back to a traditional metaphysics. However, he accepted that, in response to the Enlightenment, Christianity needed a new kind of exposition (which, in his case, is rooted in a primordial sense of a human feeling of dependence). Furthermore, though he was in no way a supporter of "individualism" (considering, for example, his insistence that, despite our individual differences, an aspect of humanity that he emphasized, we all need to participate in human society [para. 10]), his principal criticism of Catholicism is that it makes people's relationship to Christ dependent on their relationship to the church, rather than, as in Protestantism, people's relationship to the church being dependent on their relationship to Christ (para. 24). The result is an emphasis on individual responsibility that questions the authoritarian nature of churches outside the liberal tradition.

My reservations about Schleiermacher's relationship to the tradition with which I am concerned can also help to explain my reservations about what is sometimes called "postliberal theology," a movement that takes many forms and is alive and well in many theological schools, both Catholic and Protestant. Key to the central issue, as I see it, is my reference to the kind of universal rationality that the early apologists, such as Clement and Origen, believed to be found within Greek thought, and which they wanted to harness for the promotion of the gospel (in contrast to Schleiermacher's much more contextual view of rationality). Despite all kinds of variations in approach, those associated with postliberalism (and, equally, postmodernism) tend to emphasize how what we consider to be rational is hugely, if not totally, influenced by our cultural setting and our language. There is no "metanarrative" in terms of which the Christian faith, or any other system of beliefs, can express eternal truth. Similarly, for George Lindbeck, the beliefs of a religion are "cultural-linguistic" rather than "propositional."[22]

---

22. George A. Lindbeck, *The Nature of Doctrine* (London: SPCK, 1984), pp. 20-21, 30-41. Lindbeck contrasts "cognitive," "experiential-expressive," and "cultural-linguistic" models of religious thought. While differing from Lindbeck in many ways, I agree that

Though I too see revelation as a matter of propositional truths, I do not think that the "cultural-linguistic" approach to religion is adequate, and I am arguing, against the grain of much recent thinking in the philosophy of religion, that even though reasoning is *influenced* by its cultural setting and by its linguistic context, there is a genuine universal core to what we properly term the rational, of the kind explored in the next chapter.[23] For example, any adequate account of rationality must include the procedural criterion of listening to the other side *(audi alteram partem)*, some measure of consistency, and the marking of certain distinctions (such as between mathematical and empirical truths). The situation, I suggest, closely parallels the free-will debate, in which any sensible defense of free will — in addition to an attempt to elaborate its meaning — admits that we are *influenced* by all kinds of pressures, both external and internal to the mind, but that this obvious truth does not lead to the conclusion that these influences are totally deterministic. If they are, it is very difficult to make sense of either our apprehension of scientific truth or our moral intuitions. The result of this belief in a measure of universal rationality is that the kind of liberal theology that I am promoting is actually surprisingly conservative in at least two ways: not only does it uphold the Apostles' Creed, but it upholds the endeavor of the first apologists to see God's word as manifested in a *logos* (or rationality) that has a universal appeal.

In the light of this relative conservatism, I anticipate that some readers will be critical of my use of the adjective "liberal," and of my claim that it stands for a substantive, identifiable tradition from the time of the first apologists to the present day. I fully admit that many people now use the word "liberal" in a much looser way; but I suggest that in doing so they tend to lose sight of a powerful mainstream version of the Christian faith that has a genuine continuity and that — particularly in the nineteenth century — used the word "liberal" to identify a coherent stream of philosophers and theologians who responded to each other and to the

revelation is rarely, if ever, in the first instance propositional. In the New Testament and in Christian experience, it is the *person* of Jesus that is revealed, and propositions concerning him are secondary.

23. See, esp., the third volume of Gary Dorrien's *The Making of American Liberal Theology.*

themes that I shall be discussing. Perhaps, as I have suggested, the term "liberal orthodoxy" could come to be used for the tradition I describe and the general term "liberal" for versions of nonmainstream Christianity; but I would not recommend the second half of this suggestion, because the word "liberal" could even more evidently become a kind of catchall for a hugely diverse range of views. Against the grain, I would prefer to resurrect an earlier use of the term "liberal." In the context of the tradition that I outline in this book, to which I apply the word "liberal," Schleiermacher and many other prominent writers, including Ritschl, should be considered as important influences on the liberal tradition — but not as typical exemplars of it.[24]

I shall close this introductory chapter by referring to a common criticism of liberal theology to which, I believe, liberals like me should pay attention. Whatever one thinks of more conservative forms of Christianity, both Catholic and Protestant, they are sometimes combined with an active commitment to a way of life that is transforming — both of the persons directly involved and, in some cases, of the communities they touch. The problems that I identify with conservative forms of Christianity are, first, that some of the beliefs are rationally suspect, and second, that the same enthusiasm that can lead to change for the good can also, when it becomes "fanatical," lead to intolerance and a change for the worse, as demonstrated by the Inquisition of the past and the persecution of gay people in the present. For liberal Christians, the problem is to maintain both their rational reflection within the realm of theology and their humane approach to social problems, while at the same time emulating the personal warmth and courageous enthusiasm for social jus-

---

24. Albert Ritschl (1822-1889) is frequently referred to as a liberal theologian, whereas, given the nature of the tradition I describe, he should be counted as an influence but not an exponent. Partly under the influence of Kant, his emphasis is on the moral voice of Christianity, and he downplays all metaphysical content and all natural theology. By contrast, while a concern with morality is a constant feature of the liberal tradition I describe, the significance of the claim "God is good" is upheld precisely because we have some capacity to *understand* the good — a theme that goes back to Plato. Natural theology, indeed, needs to be rethought, and a much more careful account needs to be given of what counts as "argument" or "proof." But Peter's demand to give a "reason" for the faith that is in us is more than a call to a personal experience (though that may well be included).

tice that is found in both Catholic and evangelical churches when they are at their best. When liberally minded Christians see their faith primarily in terms of being disciples of Jesus Christ, charged with bringing his message of love to the world, I believe that this can and does happen. We normally associate the expression "born-again Christian" with membership in one of the more evangelical or charismatic versions of Christianity. But I can see no reason why some of those Christians who identify themselves with the liberal tradition that I describe (regardless of their denomination) could not also see themselves as born-again Christians on the grounds that becoming a disciple of Jesus has dramatically turned their lives around.

CHAPTER TWO

Eleven Typical Characteristics of the Liberal Tradition in Theology

—⊗⊗⊙—

A. Introduction

Philosophers have come to realize (partly from the teaching of Wittgenstein) that many words can only be understood, not from one single characteristic that defines all cases, but from a set of typical characteristics, which, like family resemblances, link the different uses of a word together. So far as I know, Wittgenstein did not himself apply this to the word "religion," but that is a term that brings together a number of belief systems or ways of life that typically have several things in common, such as a reverence for certain "holy" writings and people and places, some kind of ritual activity, some kind of priesthood or eldership, and so on. However, no one thing can be found in every example of what we usually consider to be a religion. The closest to a universal characteristic is probably a commitment to "a way of life" (corresponding to the *Dao* of many Eastern religions); however, that characteristic can also be applied to some "ways" that are usually considered secular. Not all religions believe in a personal God, and not all of them have holy writings and people and places — or any of the other typical characteristics.[1] Similarly, rather than emphasizing one thing as defining the liberal tradition in theology,

---

1. This applies most clearly to some nonliterate, indigenous cultures.

it is better to indicate a series of typical characteristics that I shall describe under eleven headings. Some of these characteristics, needless to say, can be found in other traditions. For example, there is often a "rational" emphasis (characteristic 2) within forms of Roman Catholicism that are certainly not liberal in terms of many of the other typical characteristics. However, when all or nearly all of these eleven characteristics are present, we can suspect that we are dealing with an example of the liberal tradition.

Among other advantages, this approach makes sense of the discovery that there is often a fuzzy line between uses of a word. Consistent with this, we find cases (such as that of Marxism) where we are not sure whether or not a movement should be called a religion because it has only two-thirds, say, of the commonly found characteristics.[2] Similarly, there are cases where whether or not a person or a teaching should be called liberal is not clear. This simply reflects the nature of human language and the way we often lump things together in words that cover a range of meanings. This is not a fault of language, for without this ambiguity we would need a hugely inflated vocabulary, which would be unhelpful; in addition, some of the interconnections between different aspects of human experience would not be so evident.

The eleven typical characteristics can be listed as follows, though variations in this list are perfectly possible. The selection owes something to my own interests, but I believe that it captures the essence of an important and recognizable tradition. I should add that, given the historical nature of this essay, except in the case of the eleventh issue, I am here especially concerned with the tradition up to about 1900. In the next chapter (under the subheading "Twentieth-century Themes") I shall indicate the importance of some additional issues that have arisen in recent years, including those of the ministry of women and of an adequate response to contemporary science and contemporary forms of capitalism.

2. Shortly after the communist revolution in China, a delegation came from that country to London. At Highgate Cemetery, as they approached the tomb of Karl Marx, they all took off their shoes. This is one of many examples of how Marxism has holy places and holy people, in addition to holy books such as *Das Kapital* and Mao's "Little Red Book" (essentially, "holy" means "set apart").

Eleven Typical Characteristics of the Liberal Tradition in Theology

(1) A Use of the Bible That Is Not Always Literal

With respect to interpretation of the Bible, the liberal approach (as it came to be called after 1781) is controversial. Many theologians in the early church were much less concerned with the literal meaning of the biblical text than is often assumed, and an emphasis on a very literal reading of the text, along with a doctrine of *verbal* inspiration, is more a feature of conservative theologians — in both Catholic and Protestant traditions — in post-Reformation times.[3] According to more conservative Christians, especially in the Protestant traditions, the pure word of God that has been given to us in the Old and New Testaments is being adulterated or undermined by alien ideas. Greek philosophy and other forms of rational discussion should not be put alongside Scripture. In contrast, those who would later be referred to as liberals have supported an element of personal freedom in the way in which Scripture should be interpreted. Indeed, Keith Ward, in his contribution to a set of essays entitled *The Future of Liberal Theology,* sees "conscientious freedom of interpretation" as the most significant hallmark of what liberal theology stands for.[4] And, though I have suggested that we should think of a cluster of "typical characteristics" as describing the nature of the liberal tradition rather than identifying a single "defining characteristic," if I were forced to pick one characteristic as the most influential, I would choose this one as well.

In response to more conservative approaches to Scripture, liberals have tended to reply with these challenges:

(a) *No text interprets itself.* When the Old or New Testament is read by anybody, he or she interprets it in accordance with certain ideas and a certain underlying philosophy. The liberal is more open and more aware than many others are about how this interpretation is taking place. In terms of authority, the "primacy" of Scripture is accepted by most liberals, provided that we are aware that it does not interpret itself. Strictly speaking, moreover, for Christians the primacy is to be found in the per-

---

3. A doctrine of verbal inspiration is explicit in Leo XIII's encyclical *Providentissimus Deus* (1893) and in many declarations of the Pontifical Biblical Commission, established in 1902.

4. Keith Ward, "The Importance of Liberal Theology," in Mark D. Chapman, ed., *The Future of Liberal Theology* (Aldershot, UK: Ashgate, 2002), p. 40.

son of Jesus rather than in the writings that bear witness to him. The uniqueness of the Bible lies in the fact that, with the possible exception of a few passages in the later "apocryphal gospels," it is the only written source for the life and character of Jesus.[5]

At this point it is important to emphasize how strong the manuscript evidence for the New Testament is in comparison with equivalent evidence for most historical events prior to the systematic keeping of records in the later Middle Ages, a situation that is often neglected by those who maintain that the life of Jesus is basically myth. If, as most independent scholars agree, the Gospels were written in the first century (with the possible exception of the Gospel of John), it is astonishing to find a fragment of John's Gospel that is dated by most scholars at about 125-150 CE (P52) and almost all the books of the New Testament from 200 CE or shortly thereafter (primarily in the collections known as the Chester Beatty and Martin Bodmer papyri). In other words, we have extant manuscripts that are copies made within about one hundred years of the original holographs.[6] This compares with a gap of hundreds of years between a host of actual events in the ancient world that are generally accepted without question, as well as the dates of the earliest manuscripts describing them. Needless to say, this does not prove the historical accuracy of all the biblical stories, but it places the New Testament record in a setting that demands serious attention. (In this regard, we should also note Richard Bauckham's recent scholarly study entitled *Jesus and the Eyewitnesses*.)[7]

Difficulties in interpreting the Bible have led many Christian writers to emphasize the different kinds of writing that are found within it, including the extensive use of metaphor, poetry, and parable — none of which make sense if taken literally. Often there are clear indications that a kind of parable is intended rather than a literal reading. For example, in the creation story in Genesis, the word "adam" (or its derivatives) is used,

5. Probably the most interesting of these is the Gospel of Thomas, which exists in a fourth-century Coptic version that is thought to be based on a second- or, just possibly, first-century collection of the sayings of Jesus. The vast majority of the apocryphal gospels are much later and are important for indicating religious thought in the second to fourth centuries, but are of little if any relevance to the historical life of Jesus.

6. A holograph is the original manuscript in the handwriting of the author.

7. Richard Bauckham, *Jesus and the Eyewitnesses* (Grand Rapids: Eerdmans, 2006).

when it was well-known by the original readers that this had three meanings in Hebrew: a "human person," a proper name, and "earth" *(adamah).* The story includes a play on the interconnection of these three senses of the word and provides a powerful message about the meaning of life. When it is read as literal history, not only does the original meaning tend to get lost, but a completely unnecessary conflict arises with the findings of scientists and historians.

(b) If there is a personal God, why should we believe that he has *only* spoken through the writers of the Old and New Testaments? Why can he not also have spoken through many other traditions, including the other world religions, especially when we find many things in common between these different traditions (such as various formulations of the golden rule that "we should treat others as we would have them treat us")? Also, why cannot God also speak to people when they use the intellects he has given them? If there is a certain kind of uniqueness in Christian Scripture, this does not entail a dismissal of scriptures within other traditions. Moreover, the liberal Christian tradition, while acknowledging the unique authority of the Bible, tries to apply the same kind of rational inquiry and sense of literary criticism that we should apply to all other books.[8] Surely, if the Bible is inspired, it ought to be able to stand up to this kind of inquiry?

Ideally, the discussion of this matter requires an exploration of what we mean by "personal" when we apply this word to the God who is said to be revealed in the Bible, an exploration that I have begun elsewhere.[9] Essentially, a personal God is one who is aware of and can have a relationship with individuals, in contrast to both Plato's "Idea of the Good," who is in no way personal, and Aristotle's "God," who is personal in some ways, because he can be happy, but not personal in the crucial matter of being able to know individual human beings (which Aristotle thought would demean him).

Sometimes the foregoing approach to the interpretation of Scripture

---

8. John Tulloch, in his wide-ranging *Rational Theology and Christian Philosophy in England in the Seventeenth Century* (Edinburgh and London: Blackwood, 1872), vol. 1, p. 27n, credits Arminianism with influencing liberal Anglicanism to take this approach.

9. See Michael J. Langford, *Unblind Faith,* 2nd ed. (Tunbridge Wells, UK: Parapress, 2010), pp. 20-21.

is attacked by more conservative believers on the grounds that liberals are "picking and choosing" texts, or interpretations of texts, according to their own agendas. There are two halves to the response. The first is to admit that a process of selection or emphasis has indeed been made, but not arbitrarily; instead, it is because the Gospels are taken to be the climax of the biblical revelation. For example (to take a theme that will recur in this book), the apparent justification of the killing of women and children of the enemy in the book of Joshua is "trumped" by the teaching of Jesus on loving our enemies. As Hannah Barnard insists, in Joshua we read what people of the time believed that God commanded, not what he actually commanded. The second rejoinder is to point out how much conservative interpreters also pick and choose, but almost always without the same acknowledgment that they do so. For example, those who quote 1 Peter 3 ("Wives, be in subjection to your husbands") rarely conform to the next verses of that chapter, which prohibit the plaiting of hair or the wearing of gold jewelry or fine clothes — let alone a host of Old Testament rules, such as putting to death those who curse their parents (Exod. 21:17). The "liberal" interpreter, who sets aside such commands on the grounds that they are not in accord with the spirit of the Gospels, is, I would claim, both more consistent with and closer to the gospel message.

(2) Reason and Revelation in Harmony

Closely connected with the nonliteral reading of many texts is an emphasis on the role of reason, since it is reason that allows us to sift and to consider the meaning of biblical passages. The events and teachings of the Bible are usually described as revelation, but not only do we use reason to interpret what we read, the truths revealed — so it is believed — are not contrary to either the rules of logic or the basic content of our ordinary moral intuitions. As the matter is often put (echoing the words of Aquinas), faith may sometimes "go beyond" reason, but it never "goes against" it.[10] Moreover, in practice, even those who claim to dismiss the claims of

---

10. Aquinas, *Summa contra gentiles,* trans. A. C. Pegis, 5 vols. (London: University of Notre Dame Press, 1975), 1:7.

reason tend to rely on it, at least covertly, because almost certainly some kind of reasoning underlies the particular interpretation they apply to a text. The importance of reason in the interpretation of revelation is still more evident if we accept the claim that the kinds of religious experience that are typically proposed as candidates for a divine Word are usually not literally "words" but events, or powerful sensations, or (as in the case of Jesus) a person. The giving of the divine "name" ("I am that I am," Exod. 3:14) is exceptional, whether it dates from the time of Moses or later, because in nearly all other cases it seems much more natural to think of prophets as those who believe that they have encountered God in some experience or some event, and who then try to describe this in their own words. (I will revisit the issue of verbal inspiration during the vignettes on Sebastian Castellio, John Smith, and Hannah Barnard in chapter 3, and again in chapter 4.)

However, we must admit that, from a Christian perspective, there are problems with this emphasis on reason. One of them concerns the realization that, if we take seriously the idea of a God who transcends space and time, we not only cannot expect to "comprehend" the divine, if God is in any sense "personal" (i.e., having a relationship with us), but there may be occasions when God's call or vocation to us "transcends" or "goes beyond" the categories that succeed, at least most of the time, in describing other relationships. Whether or not they are historical, God's encounters with Abraham and Job, to mention just two, form an integral part of the literature of both Judaism and Christianity, and neither religion can be properly understood if we do not make room for such experiences. Referring to the call of Abraham, the Bible describes how "he went out, not knowing whither he went" (Heb. 11:8, AV). However much one emphasizes the role of reason and reflection, any attempt to describe Christianity — or any of the other great religions — without taking into account the role of religious experience, and particularly the sense of a "presence," is simply not dealing with the human experiences to which religions are a response. Consequently, what I would call a sustainable version of liberal theology cannot be "a religion within the limits of reason alone" (as in one of Kant's works), but must rather emphasize the role of reason wherever it seems possible and appropriate.

This last observation prompts a suggestion with regard to a response by liberal theologians to the likes of Kierkegaard. His account of how the "knight of faith" must be prepared to "suspend the ethical" in response to the call of the divine absolute fills many liberals with alarm, because we have so often been presented with fanatical forms of religion that justify all kinds of slaughters and other evils in the name of a (supposed) divine call. My suggestion is that, though we are right to be wary of claims to a divine call, and need, as it were, to balance any apparent vocation with a belief that God is good (in a sense of "good" that is recognizable by us), at the same time we must be open to the serious possibility that there is a divine encounter that surprises and dismays. Kierkegaard's point is not just silliness; it is an exaggerated expression of an aspect of the great religions that we have to take seriously.

A second — and related — problem is that not everyone understands the same thing when we speak of "reason." As a beginning to the clarification of its meaning, I suggest the following typical characteristics for what we call reason or rationality.[11]

(a) A position is rational, or in accordance with reason, when it is as consistent as we can make it. This involves both "internal consistency," that is, coherence within the system of beliefs that we have, and "external consistency," that is, an absence of contradiction by experience and observation.[12] The expression "as consistent as we can make it" needs to be emphasized. In the hard sciences we frequently use models that help us understand certain aspects of nature, even though they appear to contradict each other. It would be highly misleading to say that, consequently, nature is in itself paradoxical, because, as John Polkinghorne puts it, "One might think of a [scientific] model as being a coarse-grained representation, applicable in a limited domain." Hence, "[w]ave-and-particle is an example of a complementary pair of models, apparently contradictory but saved from disaster by being applicable in mutually exclusive circumstances."[13] There is a parallel here to the way in which,

11. I have expanded on this problem in Michael J. Langford, *A Liberal Theology for the Twenty-first Century: A Passion for Reason* (Aldershot, UK: Ashgate, 2001), pp. 13-22, 39-64.

12. See D. D. Raphael, *Moral Philosophy* (Oxford: Oxford University Press, 1981), p. 6, for a discussion of this kind of double coherence.

13. John C. Polkinghorne, *Reason and Reality* (London: SPCK, 1991), pp. 22, 25.

within theology, we are sometimes forced to use doctrines or metaphors that sit uneasily with each other, for example, accounts of God's grace and providence over against accounts of human freedom and responsibility for the world. However, I am arguing that, for the rational person, such tensions, or "apparent paradoxes," can only be accepted as interim positions, as the best we can come up with now, positions that we are forced to adopt because we recognize limits to human understanding, and, at the same time, situations in which different aspects of human experience force us to say things that appear to be in tension.

(b) Reason enables us to be aware of different possibilities and different explanations for an event or an observation, often by the use of the imagination. This reflects one of the ways in which there is a creative aspect to reason. According to Coleridge, imagination in its primary mode is "the living power and prime agent of all human perception."[14]

(c) Reason, especially in its creative mode, enables us to see patterns in things or events — as when a picture suddenly emerges from a mass of dots.

(d) While reason may give us grounds for accepting the role of certain kinds of "authority," because they are necessary for communal human life, authority is systematically distrusted as a ground for truth. It is noted that very often people have been taught to believe opposite things, solely on the grounds of authority. Here there is an aspect of rationality that goes right back to Socrates and his paradoxical claim that he was indeed the wisest man (as the oracle at Delphi had said) because "he knew that he knew nothing." Obviously, this claim is both ironic and paradoxical (because knowing that we know nothing is, in a sense, to know something), but the power of his position lies in the rejection of authority as a guarantee of truth. We have to find out things for ourselves, and in this insight lies the beginning of both what we call science and critical philosophy. Once again, this position needs to be expressed carefully. In many areas of life, for example in science and history and ancient lan-

14. S. T. Coleridge, *Biographia Literaria*, ed. J. Engell and W. J. Bate (Princeton, NJ: Princeton University Press, 1983), pp. 304-5. In its secondary mode, imagination is "an echo of the former." Both modes are contrasted with "fancy," which is "no other than a mode of memory emancipated from the order of space and time." In ordinary language (as distinct from Coleridge's usage), the distinctions are often less sharp.

guages, we recognize that some people have an expertise that allows them to speak with "authority." This is why I use the phrase "systematically distrusted" rather than "generally rejected."

Behind these four aspects of rationality there is the recognition that sometimes what we call reason works through a process that goes step by step in order to reach a conclusion (a process that is sometimes called "discursive"), while at other times it works by a kind of leap, or "intuition," as in the example just given, when a pattern of dots ceases to be random and is suddenly seen as a whole picture.[15] What we call "deductive reasoning" in mathematics typically goes step by step as we work through a calculation, but it may also involve a leap, as when a child suddenly sees that three and four *must* add up to seven, or that Pythagoras's theorem is conclusive. Similarly the "inductive" reasonings of the physical sciences typically proceed step by step; but again, there may also be a sudden leap, for example, to a realization that hypothesis X best fits the pattern that is emerging.

In addition to deduction and induction, any comprehensive account of reason has to include the activity known as "judgment." Here, once again, there can be a step-by-step process as well as a kind of leap. A typical example is when a judge decides how long a sentence to give someone who has been found guilty of a crime. The parameters are set (in this case) by precedent and statute — say, somewhere between three and five years in prison; but exactly what sentence is best suited to a particular case is precisely where the *judge* is at work, taking into account the special circumstances of each case. Reason does not dictate that the correct answer is, say, exactly four years; but once the decision has been made, an indication that the judgment is "reasonable" is that it is likely to be upheld on appeal. In the appeal process the "reasons" leading to the act of judgment will be weighed in a way that, once again, may include both a step-by-step analysis and a sudden appreciation of a whole picture.

From this brief account of the nature of reason, it is clear that there can be no short and simple account of what it is; yet, at the same time,

---

15. John Milton is among those who contrast discursive and intuitive reason, e.g., in *Paradise Lost*, ed. W. Kerrigan, J. Rumrich, and S. M. Fallon (New York: Modern Library, 2007), 5:488.

"being reasonable" is not a purely subjective expression, with no genuine way of being able to distinguish the reasonable from the unreasonable. There is room for disagreement in detail, but much of the time there are clear criteria for distinguishing reasonable from unreasonable positions.

In making this claim about reason and rationality, the liberal tradition is at odds with several powerful contemporary movements that deny any truly universal form of rationality. The title of Alasdair MacIntyre's influential book *Whose Justice? Which Rationality?* by itself bears witness to this contemporary perspective (though I must point out that in this extremely perceptive work MacIntyre does, in the end, allow for criteria by which one form of rationality might properly be preferred to others).[16] In response to this denial of a universal rationality, many theologians have made what I consider to be a disastrous retreat, basically accepting that there is indeed no possibility of a universal, open dialogue with all people of good will, and claiming (as does the influential theologian George Lindbeck) that theological language is a distinctive "form of life." Such an approach succeeds in protecting many theological claims from secular criticism but at the cost of making them incoherent and irrelevant to the ordinary person. Christian apologetics tends to become, in effect, a form of preaching instead of a form of dialogue. This is one of many matters in which the kind of liberalism I support is in line with a key ingredient of the philosophy of Thomas Aquinas, despite some matters of disagreement with that great thinker. Divine grace is not something that is in competition with human nature (and, by implication, basic human rationality); rather, it is something that completes and fulfills it.[17] Human reason may not be adequate for anything like a full understanding of the divine, but we follow it as far as we can, and in doing so we encourage a serious dialogue with all people of good will.

As I have already suggested, it does not follow from this emphasis on reason that there is no need for revelation — that is, the disclosure by God of truths — in events or in a person or in writings. If God is a reality,

16. Alasdair MacIntyre, *Whose Justice? Which Rationality?* (London: Duckworth, 1988).

17. "Gratia non tollat naturam sed perficiat." *Summa Theologiae,* ed. Thomas Gilby, 60 vols. (London: Eyre and Spottiswoode, 1964), 1a, Q1, A8, ad 2.

it would indeed be unreasonable to deny that there could be such disclosures. The claim is that there needs to be a balance of reason and revelation; how this balance is to be achieved can best be seen from examples, as in the accounts of important writers within the tradition.

This introduction to the concept of reason can be strengthened by remembering that some difficult concepts can often be understood by contrasting them with their opposites — in this case, "irrationality."[18] Despite the difficulties found in providing a simple yet adequate account of the "reasonable," we can, in practice, usually discern manifest cases of the unreasonable, especially when a *process* of inquiry is unreasonable. For example, both philosophers and lawyers have rightly emphasized the need to listen to the other side in any serious debate: *audi alteram partem.* Even in a student essay, if the student is defending a serious claim, he or she must consider the most obvious and the most telling arguments that are likely to be made for an alternative position. (My argument here parallels that of Karl Popper, who argues that a rationalist attitude "leads to the view that we must recognize everybody with whom we communicate as a potential source of argument and of reasonable information. . . ." This, in turn, leads to a connection between the rational and the moral, because of the need to take argument seriously.)[19]

The foregoing account of the relationship of faith to reason leaves out at least one important issue. What should happen when humans receive what they hold to be a divine revelation that appears, at least on the surface, to be *contrary* to what is rational?

In order to respond to this question, let us revisit Kierkegaard's "knight of faith" and the concern that it has sometimes been in response to religious experiences that people have believed absurd things and

18. In the third book of Aristotle's *Nichomachean Ethics* (trans. H. Rackham, Loeb series [London: Heinemann, 1926]), when he wants to illuminate the notion of voluntary action, he begins by contrasting it with "involuntary action," which is easier to describe.

19. Karl Popper, *The Open Society and Its Enemies,* 5th ed. (London: Routledge and Kegan Paul, 1995), pp. 455, 470. Elsewhere, I think that Popper is too ready to characterize the "mystical" as "irrational." Mystical experience itself, in my view, is better described as "nonrational," a special kind of human experience that only becomes a source of either the rational or the irrational when we begin to interpret it.

done evil things.[20] First, we need to distinguish the experience itself from the personal interpretation of it, for many profound experiences do not, in themselves, imply any particular truth to be believed or action to be followed. Second, if a truth is believed to be revealed that appears to contradict ordinary experience or the results of rational inquiry, we must suspect that we may have misunderstood something. There may be good grounds for going back to confirm our experience or inquiry; but if we believe that our rationality is itself a divine gift, we need some kind of good reason for laying it aside. Third, there is a difference between a call to action that is surprising and one that seems to conflict with moral principles, such as justice. In the case of the former, if there is — as I believe is sometimes the case — a genuine experience of vocation, in which people sense a call to a particular style of life, or more specific action, then we cannot rule out the possibility that the result may be surprising. Of course, such vocations need to be examined and tested, but a surprising call should not be dismissed out of hand. Indeed, part of what it means to believe in a personal God is that he has specific vocations for some of us. However, this is quite different from an apparent call to commit acts that conflict with our most fundamental moral principles, such as — in past centuries — a call to burn unbelievers alive, or — in present times — a call to perform terrorist acts in which innocent bystanders will be killed. Some of our moral intuitions may be inadequate or wrong, and we should allow for the possibility that a divine revelation could help us realize this; but if there is an apparent call to disregard a basic moral principle (such as treating people as ends in themselves), then I suggest that we should doubt whether we have interpreted matters correctly.

Behind this third claim is an important Christian doctrine: God, we say, is "good." If this claim is meaningful, and not just a platitude, it means that at least the basic aspects of goodness, such as justice (which first comes to be understood in the context of human interactions), must apply to God. If a missionary tells a follower of some primitive tribal religion that God is good (as opposed to, say, the Ammonite god named Moloch, who demanded the burning of children), the word "good" carries at

---

20. See Søren Kierkegaard, *Fear and Trembling* (1843), trans. Walter Lowrie (London: Campbell, 1994).

least some of its human meaning. In fact, in the early days of Christianity, what happened is that the personal God of the Old Testament, who was sometimes portrayed as something other than good and just, was united with Plato's Idea of the Good. This mixture of Hebrew and Greek ideas has introduced interesting philosophical difficulties; however, the move was basically "creative" in the best sense of the word. If it is neglected, then a dangerous divorce between our fundamental moral sensitivities and our sense of the divine becomes possible. Sadly, the history of Christianity, and that of many other world faiths, shows what can happen when such a divorce occurs.

(3) A Nonlegalist Account of Redemption

The early Christians were convinced that they were redeemed or saved by what Christ had done through his life and death and resurrection. They believed that through him they were made "one" with God — and hence the belief in atonement (i.e., "at-one-ment"). However, though various metaphors were used, such as Jesus being a "ransom" for our sins (Mark 10:45), there was no one theory concerning how this redemption was achieved. Later, several theories developed, and one in particular — called the "substitution" theory, based in large measure on the writings of Anselm (1033-1109) — became popular in both Catholic and Protestant churches. In its cruder form (and I must emphasize that not all supporters of this theory put the matter so crudely), Jesus, on the cross, was our "substitute," paying in his suffering and death the penalty that properly belongs to us because of our sins. The justice demanded by God is thus satisfied, because Jesus has paid the price for us.

Many profoundly religious people, not to mention atheists and agnostics, have great difficulties with this way of expressing the atonement. It is certainly true that love often makes people suffer for their friends, and that through generous acts of suffering, friends are sometimes helped. Moreover, these very human experiences find a strong resonance with the picture of Jesus on the cross. For this reason, liberal Christians do not deny that Jesus died on the cross for us; but they do deny that a simple substitution theory really explains this, because as an account of how we are redeemed, it presents serious problems. For example, can a demand of absolute justice (assuming there is such a demand) really be satisfied if someone else absorbs the punishment that should be borne by the culprit? Also, if the ultimate concern of love is the reform of the sinner, how is it that allowing someone to die in our place brings about our reform? In the next chapter we shall see that Abelard gives a very interesting answer to the second question, but it is one that differs strongly from substitution theory as it is typically expressed.

Notwithstanding this criticism of substitution *theory*, the way in which the language of substitution, as used by many Christians, can succeed in conveying elements of truth, both spiritual and psychological, need not be denied. Indeed, for most Christians it is the huge symbolic power of the cross, either as seen in art or simply as held up before the mind's eye, that accounts for its spiritual significance, rather than some rationalizing about exactly how and why it can bring salvation. One of the places where this is explored is Charles Williams's novel *Descent into Hell*.[21]

The issue of how the work of Jesus brings about salvation can be clarified by contrasting the emphasis generally found in the Orthodox churches to that found in the Western churches. In the Eastern churches the emphasis is on the consequences of the incarnation, that is, the way in which the Word of God was made flesh; the cross and passion of Jesus represent the culmination and last episode in this act of God's identification with humankind. By contrast, the Western churches' emphasis has tended be on the cross and passion of Jesus, sometimes almost in isolation from the whole story. Then the rest of his life is seen as a kind of prelude to that central episode.

My preference for the Eastern emphasis can be brought out as follows. The stories of a "superman" or other heroes who have special powers, often of a magical kind, are virtually useless for the moral inspiration of ordinary people. When the going gets rough for them, unlike for us, they can fly away or catch bullets in their teeth, and so on. The real heroes who can genuinely inspire us are fellow human beings who share our vulnerability but still show amazing love or courage. Therefore, if God,

---

21. Charles W. S. Williams, *Descent into Hell* (London: Faber and Faber, 1937), chap. 6.

through a concrete example, is to show us how to live, and takes the quite extraordinary initiative of coming to be alongside us, like the Good Samaritan, he has to come as a vulnerable person, not as a superman. Then, driven by a love that seeks to identify, as far as possible, with those who are loved, God's "image" (eikon) on earth (Col. 1:15; 2 Cor. 4:4) has to share human suffering and death. Therefore, the huge importance of the cross is not on account of some bargain with the devil, nor on account of some juridical arrangement with the demands of an absolute justice, but the conclusion of a whole process that opens up a new path for us. Jesus' life is essential for us to have "the way, the truth and the life" (John 14:6), and a Christian can truly say "Jesus died for me." But strictly speaking, it is his whole life, not just the death, that works to change my heart and mind.

This point is well illustrated in the devotional writings of the influential Anglican clergyman William Law (1686-1761). Though Law was in many ways not a "liberal" (e.g., in his attack on the theater), he was a powerful supporter of the doctrine of redemption. He expressed horror at the way God is so often portrayed as disagreeable and vengeful; in contrast to the substitution theory, he saw the redemptive work of Christ as the result of a new birth within us, made possible by Jesus' identification with humankind: "[A]ll that he does for us, as buying, ransoming, and redeeming us, is done wholly and solely by a birth of his own nature and spirit brought to life in us. . . . Not a word is there said [in Scripture] of a righteousness or justice, as an attribute in God, that must be satisfied."[22] (We will revisit this issue of the nature of redemption in the section on Abelard in the next chapter.)

(4) The Possibility of Salvation Outside a Narrow Path

An illustration will help to introduce this subject. In 1643 the Anglican theologian William Chillingworth, while on his deathbed, was pressed by the Puritan Francis Cheynell to withdraw his claim that Muslims, Roman Catholics, and heretics, if they were people who genuinely endeav-

---

22. William Law, The Spirit of Love, in Works (London, 1762 [reprinted 1893]), 8:74-75.

ored to do what is good, could be saved.[23] Today his claim might seem natural, even obvious, but we need to realize how extraordinary it seemed to most people of that time, given the narrowness of so many religious people.

In the context of Chillingworth's writings, we can understand the reason for his refusal to withdraw his claim. He held the view — derived from the Alexandrine Christian tradition going back to the second and third centuries — that people who truly respond to God's *Logos* (or "Word"), as it comes to them in the form of the Good, the True, and the Beautiful, are indeed responding to the *Logos*. Christianity is unique in articulating that the *Logos* was made flesh in the person of Jesus, but this does not mean that only Christians are responsive to God's "Word." In addition to God's grace, the one absolutely essential thing required for salvation, Chillingworth claimed, is to *endeavor* to do the good, as one sees it.[24] This is to respond to the Word of God.

In Saint John's Gospel, Jesus is recorded as saying: "No-one comes to the Father except through me" (14:6); but it is also John who identifies Jesus with the *Logos,* or Word of God. From this, Chillingworth's position is easy to appreciate. All humans, whether of any other faith or none, who respond to God's Word as it comes to them in their particular circumstances, whether before or after the time of Christ, are in reality responding to the *Logos,* to the eternal Christ, whether or not they realize that this is so. It was a similar insight that allowed Justin Martyr, writing in about 151-155 CE, to claim that "those who live with the *logos* are Christians, even though they have been called atheists."[25]

I prefer to put the situation differently from the way Justin put it, and to call only those people "Christians" who not only respond to the *Logos* of God but who also articulate their belief that the *Logos* was made flesh

23. F. Cheynell, *Chillingworthi Novisssima* (London, 1644; 1725), p. 44; see also R. R. Orr, *Reason and Authority* (Oxford: Clarendon Press, 1967), p. 163.

24. William Chillingworth, *The Religion of Protestants* (Oxford, 1638), 3, 14, p. 135: "[I]f we do indeed desire and endeavour to find the truth, we may be sure we do so, and be sure that it cannot consist with the revealed goodness of God, to damn him for error, that desires and endeavours to find the truth" (cf. 2, 104, p. 92, and 3, 52, pp. 158-60).

25. Justin Martyr, *First Apology,* trans. T. B. Falls (Washington, DC: The Catholic University of America Press, 1948), p. 46.

in Jesus. Otherwise, we can easily use the word "Christian" so loosely that every decent person gets included. Also, honesty compels me to admit, with sadness, that many people can reasonably be *called* "Christians" who have not been — or are not presently — "decent persons." If we are to be consistent, then the claim that Christianity involves a commitment to follow Jesus, plus an articulation of the claim that "Jesus is Lord," leads to the conclusion that the Christian community is made up of both wheat and chaff. No doubt some of the chaff consists of people who never really intended to be disciples of Jesus, and then there is a case for saying that they are not really Christians. However, the human situation is complex, and I contend that there are some people who really intend to be disciples, but who fail to be, in any ordinary sense of the words, "decent people." Nevertheless, we can concede Justin's main point. All those who respond to God's Word in the ways in which it comes to them are responding to the eternal Christ, and we have no right to exclude them from the promises of God. Meanwhile, Christians in the strict sense, who articulate that Jesus is Lord and Christ, have a unique opportunity to share in an extraordinary insight and in a new kind of common life. They have a special kind of joy and responsibility.

References to the Alexandrine tradition, and Origen in particular, are important, partly because some conservative Christians regard the claim that many non-Christians may be included among those who "come to the Father through me" as a recent and liberal distortion of the gospel message. I argue that there has always been, within the Christian tradition, this more liberal approach (though not, of course, one that used this term). Among many other examples, consider the following reflection on this same passage from Saint John's Gospel (14:6) by an unknown German theologian, writing in about 1350: "When therefore among the creatures the man cleaveth to that which is the best that he can perceive, and keepeth steadfastly to that, in singleness of heart, he cometh afterward to what is better and better," and eventually to "the Eternal Good."[26] Cleaving to "the best that he can perceive" is surely ech-

---

26. *Theologia Germanica*, trans. S. Winkworth (London: Stuart and Watkins, 1966), p. 130. A version of this work was found in manuscript by Martin Luther and much admired by him.

oed in Chillingworth's claim that the one absolute demand is "to *endeavor* to do the good, as one sees it."

(5) Toleration

Congruent with a more open attitude toward a variety of beliefs, those who were later called liberals disclaimed the intolerance meted out to members of other religions or denominations. The sad fact is that, while the early church argued for toleration, once it gained political influence in the fourth century, it tended, especially in the West, to become an agent of persecution itself. Between the fourth and the seventeenth centuries there were some Christians who attacked this intolerance, including Abelard, Vaso (sometimes spelled Waso, a twelfth-century bishop of Lieges), Sebastian Castellio, and Jacob Acontius.[27] But a widespread support for a measure of toleration (both in matters of religion and politics) became familiar only in certain sectors of seventeenth-century thought, Bishop Jeremy Taylor's *Liberty of Prophesying* (1647) being one famous example. Even to this day, examples of religious intolerance are easy to find; the positive change is that fewer and fewer theologians and church leaders are prepared to support it. I will revisit this characteristic of the liberal tradition in the next chapter, especially in the vignettes on Castellio and Taylor.

(6) Original Sin, But Not Original Guilt

One of the grounds for intolerance, along with a belief that there is only one sure path to avoiding hellfire, is a commonly found belief that hu-

---

27. Jacobius Acontius (Aconsio) was born in about 1500 and died in 1566 or 1567. He was an Italian jurist cum theologian cum engineer who converted to a liberal form of Protestantism. He came to England shortly after the accession of Queen Elizabeth, and he was employed there on the strength of his engineering skills (in drainage and in the fortifications at Berwick). His *Stratagematum Satanae* (1565) argues that persecution is part of Satan's strategy. English editions (under the title *Darkness Discovered*) date from 1647. (Early editions of this translation omit chapters five through eight, which were more obviously critical of Calvinism.)

man beings were born not just with "original sin" (i.e., an innate tendency or weakness, rooted in the social nature of human beings, that leads all — or almost all — to fall), but an "original guilt" (i.e., a universal state of condemnation, present even at our birth). This belief can easily lead to a frenzied desire to make sure that all of our fellow humans escape the wrath they deserve, usually by accepting the one path that, it is alleged, enables people to escape their doom.

In fact, however, belief in original *guilt* is not biblical at all, but was based partly on the Vulgate's misleading translation of Romans 5:12 in the early fifth century. Where the natural translation of the Greek goes something like "we all sin like Adam," the Vulgate renders the passage this way: "We all sin in [Adam]." This suggests that, unlike the actual words of Saint Paul, we are all born with a share of our forefathers' guilt.[28] However, since the time of Jeremiah there has been a strong biblical tradition that we are individually responsible for our wrongdoings, and that we are not to be blamed for what our forefathers have done (Jer. 31:29-34).[29]

In the next chapter we shall note how some influential liberals of the past, notably Jeremy Taylor, returned to the original biblical view, here fighting a false doctrine that was commonly found in both Catholic and Protestant teaching. It is also worth noting that in 1938 the Church of England formally questioned the idea of original guilt, while it acknowledged that the idea of "original sin" included an important truth.[30] It

28. The Vulgate translation of the verse includes the words *in quo omnes peccaverunt*. There is some dispute about how best to translate Paul's Greek, and my claim that what I suggest is the more "natural" translation is based not only on one way of reading the Greek, but also on how it is better to see this passage in the context of other biblical teachings, such as that of Jer. 31.

29. Here Jeremiah is revising an older, Mosaic view, in which collective guilt and collective punishment were accepted. The theme is repeated in Ezek. 18.

30. See the report of "The Commission on Christian Doctrine," appointed by the Archbishops of Canterbury and York (1922), *Doctrine in the Church of England* (London: SPCK, 1938), pp. 63-64. In this document, though there was not universal agreement within the commission, the Church of England suggests a doctrine of original sin that is very similar to the view generally held in the Greek Orthodox Church (which never had to rely on the misleading translation in the Latin Bible), seeing a fundamental truth in the doctrine, while distancing this from any notion of inborn guilt. The recommenda-

thereby moved toward the position that is generally held in the Orthodox churches, which never needed to rely on Jerome's fallible translation.[31]

As a context for this position on original sin, it may be helpful to review Aquinas's influential teaching. His teaching on the subject (notably in his *Summa Theologiae* 1a 2ae, Qs 81-83) has several strands. On the positive side, Aquinas normally uses the expression *peccatum originale,* which, in my view, is less suggestive of the notion of blame than *culpa originalis.* Additionally, in some passages he is sensitive to the problem of attributing guilt to infants. However, he still insists that the child can inherit sin, and he gives the example of sharing the disgrace of a forebear's crime (81, 1 *ad* 5). However, sharing disgrace *(ignominia)* is very different from sharing fault *(culpa,* or *mens rea),* which, in the subsequent discussion, is assumed to be present in the child prior to baptism (e.g., 81, 3 *ad* 2). Aquinas also emphasizes the moral weakness of human beings who are subject to the "tinder of sin" (Q 81, 3 *ad* 2), and this is in line with my own emphasis on the weakness of the human condition in the context of a kind of communal solidarity. More negatively, not only does Aquinas insist that original sin is physically inherited as a result of Adam's sin, the stain comes through the male semen, not from the woman, for if only Eve had sinned there would not have been a transmission of original sin to Adam's offspring. (Following Aristotle, Aquinas thought that the mother was basically an incubator, providing the "bodily material" but not the "seminal source" of our natures [81, 4 *ad* 3; 5 *ad* 2].) In this way, Aquinas was able to say that Jesus did not have original sin because — if one accepts a literal virgin birth — biologically he was a child of Mary but not of Joseph.

Following Aquinas, Catholic teaching has often insisted on original guilt, for example, in the Decrees of the Council of Trent, session 5 of 6/17/1546, which speaks of *reatum originalis peccati,* and in the papal bull entitled *Ineffabilis Deus* (1854), which defines and declares the doctrine

---

tions were not unanimous, but many held "that in no sense can guilt *(reatus)* be rightly attached to original sin" (p. 67). This position can be compared with the 2003 revised version of *The New Catholic Encyclopedia* (Washington, DC: The Catholic University of America Press, 2003), 10:667, which still insists on the truth of an *inherited* guilt.

31. See John Meyendorff, *Byzantine Theology* (New York: Fordham University Press, 1974), pp. 143-46, which includes a discussion of the proper translation of Rom. 5:12.

of the Immaculate Conception. It includes the statement "omnes homines [Jesus and Mary excepted] nasci originali culpa infectos." Traditional Lutheran and Calvinist teachings have usually followed the same pattern. However, more recent statements of doctrine often do not mention this official teaching; for example, the recent *Catechism of the Catholic Church* has a section on original sin that makes no reference to the guilt of infants, though it emphasizes the moral weakness of the human condition (correctly, in my view). There have been some recent attempts to distance official teaching in most Western churches from inherited guilt by claiming that *culpa* did not mean "guilt" in the modern sense. However, I think that such attempts fail to appreciate the clear meaning of the doctrine in many ancient sources, including Augustine. I suggest that it is better to admit that, for the most part, the Western churches, unlike the Orthodox churches, got this matter wrong.

The relationship of original sin to original guilt can be further understood in the light of the distinction between "shame cultures" and "guilt cultures" that has been made by many scholars.[32] During the archaic period of Greece, before about 500 BCE, the human concern was much more a matter of shame and honor than of individual responsibility and choice. In the later, classical period, there is a switch toward a greater sense of inner and private responsibility, and, with it, of what we would now recognize as personal "guilt." At the same time, the gods, including Zeus, become recognizable moral agents rather than arbitrary dispensers of good and evil. Parallel changes can be seen in Hebrew culture and in many other cultures. The change is not absolute, for vestiges of a shame culture persisted — and still persist — in many places. We can partially understand the belief in "original guilt" when we see it as a relic of a shame culture in which a kind of "pollution" can be passed on to one person or family from another.[33] I would argue that the Christian doctrine of sin goes hand in hand with a recognition of personal responsibility that emerges within a culture that thinks much more in terms of guilt than of shame.

---

32. See, e.g., E. R. Dodds, *The Greeks and the Irrational* (Berkeley: University of California Press, 1951), chap. 2.

33. See Dodds, *The Greeks and the Irrational,* pp. 35, 155-56.

There is clearly a degree of tension between the emphasis on personal responsibility and the truth that our fulfillment includes an interdependence with other people. We are "relational beings," and neither the idea of a church nor of a "communion of saints" makes sense if we look only at the individuality of persons. This, I suggest, is one of many places where we need to find a creative tension, for example, between freedom and grace, between justice and mercy. Nevertheless, my view is that within this balance the acceptance of "inherited guilt" (and the allied notion of "collective punishment") should be abandoned.

Liberal theology is sometimes criticized by more conservative forms of Christianity on the grounds that it does not take seriously enough either the Fall or the more general problem of sin. Though this may be true in some individual cases, I do not think that it is a fair assessment of the positions of any of the thirteen exemplars that I provide in chapter 3. Neither the rejection of original guilt nor the (more recent) rejection of the Fall as a single historical event implies in any way that human sin (*hamartia,* literally a "falling short of the mark") and the consequent alienation of humankind from nature, other people, and God are not to be taken with utter seriousness. The story of Adam and Eve is a powerful parable that illustrates a truth about the human condition.

(7) Belief in Free Will

Most early Christian writers claimed to believe in free will, partly because, without such a belief, our sins and failures would seem to be God's fault rather than ours. However, theologians often placed so many qualifications on our freedom that others wondered if we should really be described as free. For example, when Augustine, in the early fifth century, insisted that we all need the grace of God, almost all Christians, including those later called liberals, agreed. But when he went on to suggest that the bad angels fell *because* they were given less grace than the good angels, liberals get very uneasy.[34] This suggestion, and Augustine's other references to our total dependence on God working within us, make it

---

34. Augustine, *The City of God*, ed. J. C. Welldon (London: SPCK, 1924), bk. XII, chap. 9.

hard to explain any responsibility for sin either in angels (assuming they exist) or human beings, whose wills and actions depend on how much grace God chooses to give. The problem is still more evident with John Calvin in the sixteenth century. He, too, claimed to believe in free will, but he insisted that God knows from all eternity those for whom he has decreed eternal life and for whom damnation.

At this point the discussion gets complicated, and I shall make only two more observations.

First, the view that human beings do not need grace in order to be good is often called Pelagianism. Liberals (within the tradition that I am concerned with) also reject Pelagianism — when it is defined in this way — on the grounds that, though we might achieve a certain degree of "natural goodness" by our own efforts, even on the most optimistic view we could never merit the reward of eternal happiness by these efforts.[35] We all need God's grace — in practice, for almost all of us — even to attain a moderate degree of goodness. (As I have already emphasized, liberal Christians do not reject the doctrine of the Fall, provided that it is not seen as dependent on an historical event and *is* seen as a powerful metaphor for the human condition.) However, according to "semi-Pelagianism" (which may represent the view of Pelagius himself), though grace is essential for eternal life, we ourselves can make a genuine difference to our moral life, both by our endeavors and by our free acceptance of the grace that is offered.[36] This form of semi-Pelagianism, though often attacked by conservative Christians, does represent liberal opinion.

Second, there is a big difference between saying that God knows who will be saved because he, by an act of will, *determines* this, and in saying that God *knows* who will be saved — not because he determines it but because he sees all things from "outside time." The former view is roundly rejected by liberals, though it is held by many more conservative

35. The situation is complicated by the suggestion that "ordinary" human thinking is only possible because of a kind of divine illumination — a theme that is prominent in Augustine.

36. Pelagius was a British monk, a contemporary of Augustine, and we know most of his writings only by way of quotations in which he is attacked. Many scholars believe that these attacks tend to misrepresent his actual views.

Christians. Calvin made it clear that, in his view, our election to eternal salvation or damnation was not based only on God's foreknowledge but on an eternal divine decree. In my view this theology makes any genuine free will impossible.[37] The position of Augustine is more complex, and some of his remarks show a deep understanding of the complexity of the problem of free will.[38] Perhaps it is best to say that parts of his theory tend to be "in tension" with free will rather than (as with Calvin) "in contradiction" to it. On the question of God's absolute foreknowledge, liberals are divided. Some hold that God's eternal vision, as the Creator outside time as we know it, makes this view of omniscience possible; others think that in giving us free will, God has chosen to limit himself, not only with respect to his inability to force us to be good but also in his ability to know what all our choices will be.[39]

In the following section we shall note how carefully Aquinas describes the doctrine of omnipotence, and the second of the positions just described argues that an equivalent care needs to be taken with an adequate account of omniscience.[40]

---

37. John Calvin, *Institutes of the Christian Religion* (1536), trans. J. Allen (Philadelphia: Presbyterian Board of Christian Education, 1936), 3, 22, 8; cf. 1, 16, 8-9; 2, 3, 13; 3, 21, 5; and 3, 22, 1-6.

38. See, e.g., his sensitivity to the difficulties of saying that anything "causes" the act of will, if we are to understand what "will" means (*The City of God*, bk. XII, chap. 6).

39. Those who accept foreknowledge because of God's eternal standpoint are following a position that is made explicit, most famously, in Boethius and Aquinas. Among those who take the more radical view are followers of "process theologians" such as A. N. Whitehead and Charles Hartshorne. Liberals of this persuasion accept that an act of creation could not be "within" time, because it sets up the temporal order that we know; but they claim that God, *in his relationship with us* — by giving us genuine free will — has necessarily limited his foreknowledge.

40. In this book I am not directly concerned with the philosophical problems that arise concerning the nature and meaning of free will. I have indicated a response to these problems in a 2011 journal article in which I argue that, quite apart from questions that arise in ethics and theology, a concept of free will is essential for any adequate account of scientific rationality (Langford, "Consciousness, Freewill and Language," *Philosophy Now* 87 [November/December 2011]).

(8) A View of Providence That Respects the Integrity of the Natural Order

Taking free will seriously has major consequences for how Christians understand God's providence.[41] All Christians believe that, in some sense, God rules the world, not only because he created it but also because he acts within nature and the lives of people and history. Christ is the Alpha and the Omega of history, at work in the very act of creation, and working continuously until all things are summed up in him. However, the idea that God *directly* controls every event, including every human thought and emotion, is highly controversial. That he does so is the pious belief of many devout Christians. For example, following a plane crash I heard of a preacher who insisted that this crash had to be God's will, and that he caused it so that some of the victims could join him in heaven immediately. This is most certainly not the belief of the liberal tradition.

The liberal approach to providence is intimately connected with the response to the problem of suffering, and particularly to the famous question "Why do bad things happen to good people?" The heart of the response lies in an awareness that omnipotence is an unclear term. Even in the Middle Ages theologians used to ask, "Can God limit himself?" If he cannot, he is limited by that very fact; if he can, he is limited as soon as he makes the choice to limit himself. This point, sometimes called "the paradox of omnipotence," is not just a clever play on words; it is a way of showing that what looks like a simple idea — namely, "absolute power" — is in fact ambiguous. In choosing to make human beings, God has chosen to limit himself, because freedom is an essential part of our very nature. We see an analogue of this when, as parents, we begin to liberate our children, sometimes allowing them to do things that hurt us, because without this liberty they cannot mature.

Aquinas was among those who were particularly sensitive to the difficulties of describing the nature of God's power. He disliked any lan-

41. The original sense of the word "providence" concerns how God can foreknow what will happen, but it has come to refer, more particularly, to the way in which God governs the world.

guage that suggests that God is limited or that he "cannot" do certain things, preferring instead to claim that it is more appropriate *(convenientius)* to say that it makes no sense to speak of God either being able to break the law of noncontradiction (in other words, of doing things that are strictly illogical) or being able to do what is evil (because this would be in conflict with his loving nature). "Whatever does not involve a contradiction," he says, "is in that realm of the possible with respect to which God is called omnipotent."[42] In less guarded language, we could say that God's power is not such that he can do literally anything, and that this is one of many instances in which people who attack theism tend to attack a caricature.

This can be put another way. Just as God cannot make two plus two equal five (if we keep with the standard meaning of the terms), so he cannot *make* a bad person good, because if he were to do so, the person in question would not be a person but some kind of machine. Descartes might not have been happy with this claim, but it certainly expresses a traditional Christian view of the nature of omnipotence, based on Aquinas's account of the relationship of God's power to the law of non-contradiction.[43] God can encourage us and influence us to be good, but he cannot *make* us good. What grace can do when it works within us, encouraging us to be good, is analogous to the way in which parents and friends influence us — where we recognize a power to change our lives that, at the same time, respects our freedom.

Misunderstandings about Christian teaching concerning omnipotence help explain the rejection of Christianity among many well-intentioned and generally fair-minded agnostics and atheists. If asked to describe what "God" means in the Christian tradition, many such critics would include "omnipotence" in that description. This is quite reason-

---

42. Aquinas, *Summa Theologiae*, 1a, Q25, A3; cf. A4 and 1a 2ae, Q93, A4.

43. See Descartes's reply to the sixth set of objections to his *Meditations on First Philosophy*, trans. John Cottingham et al., *The Philosophical Writings of Descartes*, vol. 2 (Cambridge, UK: Cambridge University Press, 1984), p. 291, para. 432. "It is because he willed that the three sides of a triangle should necessarily equal two right angles that this is true and cannot be otherwise. . . ." Cf. Hugo Grotius's claim that even God "cannot cause that two times two should not make four" (*De Jure belli ac pacis* [1625], trans. F. W. Kelsey et al. [Washington, DC: Carnegie Institute of Washington, 1913-1925], I, 1, X, 5).

able. However, when they are then asked what omnipotence means, I have often found that they take it to imply, quite literally, that God "can do anything." When I suggest that such a definition renders Aquinas a kind of atheist (because he rejected this kind of "God"), I am met with great surprise. Moreover, it is worth pointing out that Aquinas's careful approach is taken, perhaps in still stronger language, by Anselm (writing nearly two hundred years earlier). In his *Proslogion* he argues that the ability to tell lies or be corrupted, or to do similar things, is not power but impotence *(impotentia).*[44] The theme returns in his *Cur Deus Homo?*, where, in the context of trying to adumbrate a rational theology, Anselm takes a bold line on the issue of lying. Some apologists had argued that "lies" that were carried out at the command of God (such as in the classical cases of the Jewish midwives and of Rahab the harlot) were not really lies. In contrast, and consistent with his overall attempt to claim that God — properly understood — always acts rationally (though often beyond our comprehension), Anselm argues: "It does not follow that if God wishes to lie, it is just to lie; rather it follows that that being is not God" *(potius Deum illum non esse).*[45] If one takes the view, as I do, that it is sometimes legitimate to tell a lie — for example, to save an innocent life, and not for one's own advantage — then Anselm's argument needs to be put more carefully. Whether or not "white lies" are sometimes permissible, if a "God" commanded one to be a generally untruthful person, then — given the intimate connection between the concepts of God and of the good — that "'God' would not be God."

In this interrelationship of the concept of God with the concept of human goodness we see a powerful example of how the blending of the Hebrew Creator-God with Plato's Idea of the Good radically affected Christian theology. God is essentially identified not just with power and will, but equally with the very idea of justice. This is one reason why Aquinas's doctrine of "the Eternal law of God," which he places before his account of natural and positive divine law, is so central. There is a kind of order or internal rationality within the very being of God, though its full

44. Anselm, *Proslogion*, trans. M. J. Charlesworth (Oxford: Clarendon Press, 1965), p. vii.

45. Anselm, *Cur Deus Homo?*, trans. E. S. Prout (London: Religious Tract Society, 1886), pp. 1, xii.

nature is beyond our comprehension. (This theme will return during my discussion of dialectical theology in chapter 4 below, where, evoking Aquinas's useful and much-neglected distinction between a *via inventionis* and a *via judicii*, I argue that human beings first discover the meaning of "good" and "just" in the context of human interaction and only later realize that God is good by some kind of necessity.)

The consequences of this more mature view of omnipotence for the doctrine of providence are clear, and they affect nature and human lives and history. Moreover, there has been a large amount of theological thought devoted to this insight within the last hundred and fifty years, especially in writings concerning the "kenotic" understanding of creation.[46] In nature, if God were directly to control every movement of every subatomic particle, there would be no laws of nature, no predictability, no science, and more importantly, no human responsibility — because, whatever we did, God would "make it all right." In human action there would be no genuine freedom and no real love. In history, every outcome would be rigorously determined, and, once again, genuine responsibility for the consequences of our actions would disappear.

According to a liberal view, God may know and control the sweep of history, because this depends on long-term causes and pressures; God may be able to control these without orchestrating every individual event. Thus the Father could foretell that, given human nature, sooner or later someone would betray the Messiah. Also, a few days before the crucifixion, Jesus "knew" that Judas would be the betrayer because he could see into his heart. However, it could not be known, say, at the time of David, who this would be. If this could be "known" (at the time of David) in any ordinary sense of the term, then it could have been communicated, for example, to a prophet. But — apart from other considerations — this, in turn, would change the situation and make the prediction uncertain.

The consequences of giving up the belief in a universal providence are not as dramatic as they might seem, for the following reason: when we fully appreciate what a difference it can make to "walk in the Spirit,"

46. *Kenosis* is the Greek word for "emptying," as when, in Phil. 2:7, God is said to have emptied himself by becoming human. For recent views on the implications of this, see esp. the contributions of Keith Ward and Paul Fiddes in J. C. Polkinghorne, ed., *The Work of Love* (London: SPCK, 2001).

then, though we need not think of God as actually arranging every event, we can see him — through our cooperation — as being active within every event. The Acts of the Apostles, for example, reads like a "saga of the Holy Spirit" because much of the time the central characters are so much in tune with God that quite extraordinary things happen. This did not require a whole series of miracles (a topic I will discuss at the end of this chapter), but an awareness of how different life can be, and is, when people are in harmony with nature, with themselves, and with the Creator.

The English philosopher Alfred North Whitehead had a powerful way of presenting a similar position. He argued that providence, in terms of human beings and human history, works by "persuasion." This may sound like a weak force, but it is not. Not only does it persist throughout our lives and despite any faults that we have, but love has the unique ability to move us while respecting our freedom. It is the power of Jesus in the manger, on the cross, and in his voice across time. This has a power to move humans in ways that no show of force can achieve. Force may make us change our plan out of fear, but it cannot change what our hearts want to do. I am not claiming that this idea of "persuasion" tells the whole story of providence, especially in the natural world, but it provides a way of seeing how providence can be compatible with freedom.

The emphasis on a providence that respects the natural order is perfectly in tune with another aspect of the thinking of Aquinas, who distinguishes the way in which every event has God as its "first cause" (because he created the natural order) but also has natural forces as its "second cause" (or "proximate" cause), and it is the latter with which we are usually concerned in practical living. This also implies that we should not blame God for every unfortunate happening, nor expect God to take over our responsibilities. As Austin Farrer put the matter, "God makes the world make itself," and this is how it has to be if we are to have the possibilities of responsibility and love.[47]

The Christian response to the presence of evil and suffering in the world deserves a much fuller treatment than I can give it here, but I shall conclude this section with a brief reflection on Voltaire's satirical book *Candide*, which in a brilliant way satirizes a form of traditional Christian-

---

47. Austin Farrer, *A Science of God?* (London: Geoffrey Bles, 1981), p. 90.

48

ity that (following Leibniz) calmly asserts that we live in "the best of all possible worlds" and that all is really well because God is fully in charge.

At several places in this book I insist that it is essential, if we are to have a rational discussion, to consider an idea or a tradition when it is represented at its best — and not by caricature; that is to say, we must "listen to the other side." For example, though I have suggested that many atheists are irrational because the forms of theism they attack are caricatures of theism at its best, I have also argued that it is possible to be a rational atheist. And even though I disagree with (rational) atheists, I respect their position and — as I have already emphasized — hold that atheism, at its best, represents one of the rational options open to the genuine searcher after truth. The relevance of this for an appreciation of *Candide* is clear. Seen as an exposure of many naive forms of Christianity, it is brilliant and effective (as well as, much of the time, full of wit). However, it is only marginally relevant to a serious discussion of Christianity at its best.

In the first place, it is one thing to say that good can, at least on many occasions, be brought out of evil; but it is a very different thing to say that God intended the evil in order to bring about the good that would follow. Some Christians, including John Calvin, do seem to believe that every event is the result of the express will of God (as do many, but not all, Muslims), but this view is a caricature of the liberal tradition. The crucifixion, or some other form of execution, may have been a virtually inevitable outcome of the life of Jesus in the context of his time, but this does not mean that the evil and suffering were "intended" in the ordinary sense of that term. Providence is often a matter of bringing good out of evil, but not a matter of the divine orchestration of all that happens. Tragedy and loss are sometimes unavoidable elements in the human drama, as the biblical saga makes clear.

With Voltaire and many other brilliant satirists, there lies behind the evident problem of caricature a genuine philosophical and theological issue that I shall discuss only briefly (because this topic rapidly becomes very technical). In ordinary language, we tend to assume that we know the meaning of the terms "best" and "most perfect." However, when we apply these adjectives to many nouns, there is a singular lack of clarity. For example, what would the most perfect "city" be like? Could it exist without a built-in capacity for change? If it could not change, then we seem to have an undesirably static city, in which, for example, there would be no new children; if it could change, what would stop it from changing for the worse (unless there is some undesirable dictatorship controlling all that happens)? Issues of this kind are magnified when we apply the idea of perfection to God, or to heaven, but they also occur when we apply it to the whole of human culture. The point is not that the term "perfect" is meaningless, but that it is exceedingly unclear. Furthermore, with respect to God, the application of the word "perfect" hides genuine differences of view. For example, traditional Christianity claims that God's perfection commits us to believing that there is an absolute "changelessness" within the essential nature of God, while some theologians challenge this.[48]

Consequently, when Voltaire refers to the idea of "the best of all possible worlds," even if we conclude that this present order is certainly not such a place in the ordinary sense of the term (because we can easily imagine a world in which there is less suffering), serious questions arise about the price that would have to be paid for having a world in which either natural forces or human will were not allowed to have their expected consequences.

(In the context of a more extended analysis of the concept of providence, I have elsewhere discussed the traditional distinctions between "general providence," "special providence," and the miraculous.[49])

(9) The Joint Need of Faith and Works

On the surface, one of the tensions between Catholic and Protestant teaching has been between the Catholic view that we can, to a degree, merit grace through good deeds and the insistence of Luther and Calvin that "all our righteousness is as filthy rags" (quoting Isa. 64:6), so that our salvation depends *entirely* on the unmerited gift of God. We are justified by faith, or, more accurately, we are justified by grace, through faith.

48. See, e.g., Charles Hartshorne, *The Logic of Perfection* (LaSalle, IL: Open Court, 1962). Hartshorne raises the question of whether God can surpass himself (p. 35).

49. Michael J. Langford, *Providence* (London: SCM Press, 1981).

An encouraging aspect of recent dialogues between Christian denominations is the way this old opposition has been seen to be based, in large part, on misunderstandings, though there remain legitimate differences of emphasis. Recent statements of accord between Catholics and Lutherans have claimed that, properly understood, there is no fundamental disagreement on this issue.

Reference to the New Testament makes it clear how both the good life and faith are deemed crucial.[50] To what extent a good life follows as a consequence of having received grace, and to what extent a good life prepares the way for receiving grace, is a complex matter on which people can express different views.[51] However, Catholics and Lutherans agree that God's love and God's grace are not dependent on our worth. Just as human parents love their children unconditionally, so God loves us despite our faults — and not because of our goodness. Overall, it is no longer necessary to see a fundamental disagreement between Catholicism and Protestantism on this matter.

The result of this newfound accord is that liberals, who have always emphasized the need for both faith and good works (e.g., in the writings of John Smith, discussed in the next chapter), no longer stand out as different from most other Christians with respect to their teaching about grace, though this was historically a distinguishing mark of the tradition. However, there remains a tension with some conservative Protestants, who are not prepared to grant any significant role to human endeavor.

(10) A Minimal Number of Basic Teachings

On this matter the tension is primarily between liberals and conservative Roman Catholics, for whom many doctrines, claimed to be "latent" in the Bible or early church tradition, are held to be *de fide* (i.e., "articles

---

50. Compare, e.g., Matt. 25:31-45 with Rom. 3:20-28.

51. The story of the Roman centurion Cornelius in Acts 10 is a good example of how God's grace sometimes comes to those who have prepared the way for receiving it through good lives. However, it is also true that sometimes grace seems to come, as it were, out of the blue. In such cases it is impossible for us to know what kind of internal preparation, if any, has taken place.

of faith"). Belief in these is required in order for one to be a good Catholic. Similarly, some — but not all — Protestant sects have developed special teachings that are held to be articles of faith for members of that sect, for example, beliefs about the manner of Christ's Second Coming. However, the more general tendency in Protestantism is to reduce the number of core beliefs.

Liberals have been strongly in favor of a minimum number of core beliefs and have tended to regard the other beliefs as, not necessarily false, but as unimportant, or perhaps secondary. Take, for example, a typical liberal attitude toward the doctrine of the Assumption of the Blessed Virgin Mary, promulgated as an infallible doctrine and an article of faith by Pope Pius XII in 1950. Most liberals, including myself, do not want to spend time and energy attempting to argue that the doctrine is untrue, especially since the argument might be distressing to those for whom the doctrine is an integral part of their spiritual life. In addition, as I shall argue in chapter 4, when it is seen as symbolism, the doctrine may contain an important truth. I must admit that there is the danger that this position may sound patronizing, but the liberal cannot see why this teaching should be placed as an "article of faith" alongside central doctrines of the faith, especially those about creation, redemption, and the Trinity. Surely, if people find secondary beliefs helpful in their personal devotions, we should simply respect that; but when they are presented as important elements in Christian teaching, we can disagree without giving reasons for our difference of opinion — unless pressed to do so.[52]

In contrast to doctrines that liberals may hold to be unimportant, there are some that they may feel to be profoundly problematic. In chapter 4, I shall consider the doctrine of the Immaculate Conception (1854), which is arguably an example of such a doctrine because of its teaching about original guilt *(culpa,* or *reatus),* which, as we have seen, the Orthodox tradition does not make a necessary element in "original sin."

---

52. There is an important complication here. Some of these "secondary" teachings may be regarded (1) as true but not central, others (2) as of doubtful truth but unimportant and basically harmless, (3) while others are teachings likely to lead us astray. An example of the last kind, for liberals, is Vatican teaching on artificial birth control as being intrinsically evil, even for married people (the teaching of the 1968 encyclical *Humanae Vitae*).

(11) A Range of Acceptable Lifestyles

In the early church there was a tendency to believe that, though the married life was acceptable, the celibate state was intrinsically more noble. I do not think that there is anything in the Gospels that supports this view; however, Saint Paul's suggestion that "if they cannot contain, let them marry, for it is better to marry than to burn [with passion]" (1 Cor. 7:9, AV) could be taken to imply a difference of status. My own belief is that this quote does not reflect any belief on Paul's part about the inferiority of the married state, but rather his conviction — at the time he wrote those words — that the end of the world was imminent and thus that Christians' first priority was to prepare for that event. However, when combined with a certain kind of Puritanism (already present — to use an anachronism — in the Greek-speaking world), it was easy for the desert fathers to promote the celibate state as something intrinsically more noble than the married state.[53] Even as late as 1954, a Vatican encyclical insists that the virgin state, when undertaken for the right reasons, is an intrinsically higher state than that of marriage.[54] Many Christians are highly suspicious of this elevation of one kind of calling above another, though most accept that celibacy is a genuine spiritual call for some men and women. (The liberals' objection to celibacy has tended to be that men and women have often been pressured into such a life at too young an age.) However, there is nothing "lower" about the expression of human sexuality, provided that, like everything else, it is in accordance with love and responsibility.

It is for this reason that most liberals assume that when the New Testament refers to the brothers and sisters of Jesus (e.g., in Mark 6:3), there is no good reason to think that these were not real siblings, that is, sons and daughters of Joseph and Mary. Some traditional Christian belief has held that not only was Mary a virgin when Jesus was born (a belief that many contemporary liberal Christians do not regard as essential for Christianity), but that she had a perpetual virginity: that is, the brothers and sisters of Jesus mentioned in the New Testament were either cousins or half

53. See Dodds, *The Greeks and the Irrational,* chap. 5.
54. The encyclical *Sacra Virginitas* of Pius XII.

brothers and sisters (for whom Joseph was the father from an earlier marriage). It is possible, though somewhat unnatural, to read the Greek in this way; but the reason for this reading is the understandable desire to raise Mary to the highest moral level. On the liberal view, there is absolutely no need for this level to be associated with perpetual virginity.[55]

In recent decades, a more relaxed approach to a range of legitimate lifestyles has taken on a new prominence because of the discussion of homosexuality. It is important to appreciate that new features of this debate are the well-founded claims (1) that homosexual activity is very common in the animal world, (2) that this activity may be "natural" in having a Darwinian explanation in terms of behavior that helps a species to survive (for example, by reducing tension among males that are excluded from the herd), and (3) a significant minority of adult human beings find that their sexual inclinations are exclusively homosexual.[56]

In the case of human beings, the extent to which homosexual orientation is biologically programmed is controversial. There is no evidence for a single gay gene, but some studies, especially those of twins reared apart (whose early environments are different), may indicate that there are genetic factors in homosexuality. However, because of scientific controversies concerning how to interpret these studies, I will leave open the possibility of genetic factors in homosexual orientation.[57] Nevertheless, the new evidence concerning sexual orientation (either because of

55. One reason for doubt concerning this issue is that the historical sources for the birth narratives (in Matthew and Luke) cannot, like the other parts of the Gospels, be directly related to eyewitnesses who were alive when the Gospels were written. Another is the view that a literal virgin birth is not necessary for a robust doctrine of the incarnation, because, if God could work through Mary, he could equally work through a human father. Yet another reason is the awareness that at the time there was a general tendency to attribute virgin births to special people. In chap. 3 we shall note how Justin Martyr refers to some early Christians who did not believe in the virgin birth.

56. For scientific data on these topics, one could begin with A. F. Dixson, *Primate Sexuality* (Oxford: Oxford University Press, 1998); F. de Waal, *Peacemaking Among Primates* (Cambridge, MA: Harvard University Press, 1989); and the scientific journal *Animal Behaviour Abstracts*. Surveys of adults suggest that somewhere around 2 percent of people have exclusively homosexual orientations.

57. Among important studies is T. J. Bouchard et al., "Psychological Differences: The Minnesota Study of Twins Reared Apart," *Science* (1990): 223-28, 250.

biology or early environment or a combination of the two) needs to be underscored. In earlier times it was understandable that people could think that all sexual preferences were matters of choice, and this encouraged the view that there could be universal rules about appropriate sexual behavior that applied to all people. Perhaps sexual rules were unnecessarily rigid in the past, but my point is that new knowledge has forced all rational people to reassess what these rules should be — whether one is Christian or not. In particular, we have to ask whether traditionalists are justified in demanding that those who, as adults, find that they have only homosexual orientations are morally bound to be celibate.

We must be careful about the implications of biological factors, if they are established. If it is the case that — for some people — a homosexual orientation is wholly or partly the result of biology (or of early environmental factors), this does not immediately lead to the conclusion that it is permissible to follow it. Many natural inclinations, such as anger, have to be tempered or managed by the virtuous person. In an extreme case, a person might find that his or her orientation is entirely toward sadistic or masochistic sex, and it is difficult to see how a good person could respond to this drive other than in seeking ways to sublimate it by routing the energy into other channels. Nevertheless, the fact that some people — again, as adults — find that they have exclusively homosexual orientations has important consequences. Traditionalists have argued that "nature" gives us *the* purpose of sexuality, namely, procreation; those traditionalists have then gone on to claim that any sexual activity that knowingly frustrates this overarching purpose must be wrong. In contrast, I am suggesting that, viewed from the perspective of scientific observation, combined with a Darwinian theory of evolution, nature seems to endow sexuality with at least two purposes, namely, procreation and the cementing of relationships that are expressions of bonding that make life happier, and that, as a result, reduce tensions (which, in turn, may sometimes help to promote procreation).

Having said the above, prior to adulthood there is a strong case for a conservative approach to both heterosexual and homosexual sexual relations, partly because of the danger of sexually transmitted diseases, partly because of the likelihood that some actions may trivialize (and thus reduce the potency of) an activity that can have the power to symbolize and seriously cement committed relationships, and, perhaps most importantly, because there is unlikely to be the wisdom to know when there is a real danger of causing hurt to another person. In the case of homosexuality, there is also the problem that young people cannot be certain of their eventual orientation, and what is done at an early age can have an impact on that.

However, with respect to adults, not all reflective Christians agree about how to interpret biblical references to homosexuality, nor on exactly what the appropriate rules concerning sexual behavior should be.[58] For example, it is one thing to approve of civil partnerships for two people of the same gender who are living in a committed relationship; it is another thing to call this "marriage."[59] In this discussion I do not propose

58. References in the Old Testament (mostly in Leviticus) run into the difficulty that many injunctions are generally thought to be obsolete or reflective of a primitive outlook (such as the demand that those who curse their father or mother should be put to death [Lev. 20:9]). The Gospels make no direct reference to the topic, and Saint Paul, esp. in Rom. 1, is thought by some commentators to be condemning (rightly) a range of Roman practices such as the sexual exploitation of children. The application to, e.g., two forty-year-olds in a lifelong, committed same-sex relationship is highly controversial. For a well-reasoned reading of these texts (with generally conservative conclusions), see Richard B. Hays, *The Moral Vision of the New Testament* (Edinburgh: T&T Clark, 1996), chap. 16. One problem with Hays's position is that, if his argument is to support a universal moral teaching (corresponding to the universal morality of Rom. 2:14-15), rather than a matter of a specifically Christian vocation (corresponding to a "positive Divine Law"), then his conclusions need to be backed with some kind of nonbiblical argument that is persuasive to non-Christians.

59. Those who call themselves liberal Christians are divided on this issue, not only for etymological reasons (of how the word "marriage" should be used), but, more significantly, on account of any implications there might be for what is considered to be the ideal societal context for bringing up children. The different arguments in this debate warrant a much more extended treatment. For a defense of the term "marriage" within same-sex unions, see William N. Eskridge Jr., *The Case for Same-Sex Marriage* (New York: The Free Press, 1996). For a serious questioning of the term — in the context of the implications for family life — see Brenda Almond, *The Fragmenting Family* (Oxford: Clarendon Press, 2006), pp. 165-68. Among the issues is that of what should count as "consummation." In the jurisprudence of traditional marriage, a failure to consummate by either party, either by intent or by impotence, has been a ground not for divorce but for nullity. I would be among those who would argue that the issue of what, if anything, should count as "consummation" is inappropriate for same-sex relationships. Perhaps this should, in the future, also apply to legal heterosexual partnerships; but to say this is

to settle these issues (especially when those of generally liberal views disagree) but only to show how and why an increasing number of Christians tend to favor the moral legitimacy of a wider range of lifestyles than were favored in the past.

One of the reasons for supporting a change in attitude is the realization of the importance of listening to different voices, even if one does not always agree with them. Formerly, it was often a case of men laying down the law about how women should behave, without listening to the voices of women.[60] Similarly, I am nervous about married people such as myself (in a traditional heterosexual union) laying down the law about how those with gay or lesbian orientations should live — without listening to their voices.[61]

However, in my view, there is one moral principle in the area of sexual relations that should be treated as an absolute, namely, that we should always treat all people as ends in themselves, not merely as means. This principle, I would argue, is an example of one of those universal parts of the moral law that Saint Paul refers to in Romans 2:14-15, which should be seen as binding on all people, be they Christians or members of another faith or secular humanists. Moreover, this principle, which is often seen as an implication of the Golden Rule, has huge practical implications for sexual and all other interpersonal relationships. For example, it is hard to see how casual or promiscuous relationships

---

to admit that there is now a significant difference to the traditional jurisprudence of marriage. An obvious complication is that even in the past when, for example, two aged people were married, physical consummation was not something that seemed to be essential. However, it might be argued that this is because such marriages were not typical of the "standard" concept of marriage. Clearly, the issues are more complex than many realize and are not simply a matter of trying to avoid inappropriate discrimination. Perhaps we should say that we are now "redefining" or "redescribing" the concept of marriage; but if this is so, we should admit the change.

60. See Carol Gilligan, *In a Different Voice* (Cambridge, MA: Harvard University Press, 1982). In this book Gilligan makes an interesting distinction between the ethics of justice and the ethics of care, a distinction that highlights (though it does not exactly mirror) the difference between male and female voices.

61. Stanley Hauerwas is an example of a theologian who seeks to listen to the voices of gay and lesbian Christians in, e.g., *Sanctify Them in the Truth* (Edinburgh: T&T Clark, 1998), chap. 6.

can possibly accord with this demand, because outside a relationship in which the other person is both known and valued, how can one be sure that the other is not being "used" as a kind of commodity? The use of another person for our own gratification, without taking into account their long-term interests, is wrong. Respect for persons lies at the heart of morality, and the Christian doctrine of love, based on both the example and the teaching of Jesus, far from rejecting this principle, gives it an even higher status.

With respect to the biblical arguments, this point must be emphasized. The "literalist" argument condemning all homosexual behavior, which depends on quoting a few verses — mostly from Leviticus in the Old Testament and from Saint Paul in the New Testament — is very unsatisfactory. Almost all Christians acknowledge that some former rules are no longer appropriate, either because they were always too narrow, or because in the light of the New Testament they no longer apply, as we see in Jesus' rejection of "an eye for an eye and a tooth for a tooth" (Matt. 5:38-39).[62] Few people now believe that those who curse their parents should be put to death (Exod. 21:17), or that it is intrinsically evil to get interest for money invested (Deut. 23:19),[63] or that an animal involved in sexual intercourse with a human should be put to death (Lev. 20:15), or that Saint Paul's strictures about women speaking in church are appropriate now (1 Cor. 14:34).

However, in addition to problems surrounding the proper interpretation of all these passages, not all biblical arguments are "literalist." There are more serious ones based on general principles found throughout the Bible rather than ones based on single verses, and one of these principles concerns the high value to be placed on marriage, for exam-

---

62. Here Jesus is directly contradicting the Mosaic rule of Exod. 21:24, Lev. 24:20, and Deut. 19:21.

63. Many like passages occur in the Old Testament. The Jews were allowed to lend money with interest to "strangers" but not to fellow Jews (or "brothers"). There has been much discussion concerning how to apply this rule in later times, and there can be legitimate variations in interpretation; but the key point is that those who do charge "brothers" (i.e., fellow Jews or Christians) interest are either rejecting the rule or interpreting it in a way that is convenient to them. This is not "literalism" in the straightforward sense of the term.

ple, in the teaching of Jesus.[64] How far this principle has implications for sexual relationships outside monogamous marriage is a matter on which there can be legitimate differences of opinion, and that is why, while they dismiss literalist arguments based on quoting single verses, not all those who consider themselves liberals have the same view. Furthermore, in addition to biblical arguments, adequate discussion needs also to consider how far and how quickly ancient traditions should be set aside, and also to investigate the health implications of some sexual practices.[65] (I will revisit some of these issues in the section on Karl Barth in chapter 4 below.)

B. A Liberal Approach to Miracles

For much of the church's history, the faith has been "proved" to nonbelievers through the alleged occurrence of miracles. For example, in the seventeenth century one of the most popular books in England was a translation of Hugo Grotius's *On the Truth of the Christian Religion,* which sought to use biblical miracles in order to establish the truth of the gospel.[66] Increasingly, the liberal tradition has backed away from this approach to faith, and the reasons for this need to be appreciated. Even though miracles were considered to be extremely important in the early days of Christianity, I shall argue that they do not provide an appropriate way of demonstrating the truth of Christianity to the present generation.

---

64. It has been suggested, e.g., that the complaint about women speaking in church refers to gossip in the gallery and not active involvement in the service.

65. In a recent lecture at Cambridge, a conservative theologian argued that homosexual activity was contrary to universal morality *because* of the (alleged) consequences of penetrative sexual activity. Presumably, if this is *the* reason why such activity is wrong — as a matter of natural law — there should be no objection to nonpenetrative sexual activity. I think it is very unlikely that this concession would be granted by most conservatives, and if I am right about this, it looks very much as if they are stretched to find a natural-law reason why all homosexual activity (within committed, loving relationships) is wrong.

66. Hugo Grotius, *The Truth of the Christian Religion,* ed. Simon Patrick (London, 1680; English translation of *De Veritate Religionis Christianae* [1627]). The first of many English editions was printed in 1632.

This does not mean miracles are unimportant — for at least two reasons: first, the symbolic force of, for example, the "first sign" at Cana in Galilee is enormous; second, as we shall see, though there may be no rational route from miracles to the existence of God, there may well be a rational route from belief in God (based on other grounds) to belief in the reality of some miracles. When this situation arises, particularly in the context of personal experiences of extraordinary events, then what are believed to be miraculous happenings may quite properly form part of someone's life story.

The first reason why miracles cannot properly be used to demonstrate the truth of Christianity to an unbeliever arises from an ambiguity concerning how the term "miracle" should be used. In the Bible the words that are likely to be translated with the word "miracle" usually mean "a marvelous act" (from the Hebrew *mopheth*), or a "sign" (from the Greek *semeion*). Gradually, as the concept of "laws of nature" developed, and with that the notion of scientific explanation, the idea arose that a miracle was something that "defied" or "suspended" natural laws, whereas, when we look at early writings, any distinction between a "naturalistic" cause (i.e., one that could be explained by natural forces) and a "miraculous" cause (i.e., one that could not) would have been much less clear. However, by the time of Aquinas (in the thirteenth century), such a distinction could be made, though perhaps not with the force that it would acquire as more and more people became accustomed to scientific methodology. Aquinas defined miracle (from the Latin *miraculum*) in its strict sense (as opposed to the more general sense of a wonder) as "something that happens outside the whole realm of created nature," and is done by God.[67] As we have seen in the discussion of providence, there is for the theist a sense in which all things are done by God, because he is the "first cause." But in the case of ordinary events, the relevant explanation is in terms of what Aquinas called "secondary" causes, which is why what we might call a "natural" explanation is possible. However, in the case of miracles, according to Aquinas, God is the "direct" cause.

When miracles refer to "marvelous acts" or "signs," there is not much dispute because nearly everyone agrees that some events are marvelous

67. *Summa Theologiae* 1a, Q114, A4.

(such as rainbows) and that some can be treated as signs (such as high barometric pressure before a storm). A different kind of amazement and a new kind of dispute arises when an event is said to "go beyond nature." In hindsight, this notion could certainly be applied to some biblical events, such as the alleged stopping of the sun (Josh. 10:12-13), but not to others. For example, many of the healing miracles might have a natural explanation in terms of psychosomatic healing. In the case of the Israelites' crossing of the Red Sea, the Bible itself suggests what we would now call a natural explanation, when a strong wind blows back the waters all night long (Exod. 14:21). (We must remember that "Red Sea" is a poor translation of the Hebrew *yam suph,* or "sea of reeds," which suggests a very shallow estuary.)

When miracle is defined in the narrower or Thomistic sense, it becomes unclear how far Christianity depends on the actual occurrence of miracles, with the exception of the resurrection as it is normally interpreted. Certainly, liberals are likely to view events like the alleged stopping of the sun in Joshua as pious legends rather than history. Creation, of course, is believed to be a divine action, but Aquinas insists that this is not a miracle in the strict sense because it is not an event *in nature*. It is something still more "marvelous" — the setting up of the whole system of nature. (Aquinas says the same thing about redemption, which, like creation, does not depend on one event "within nature.") The virgin birth would be a miracle, but, as I have already noted, many Christians do not regard it as important, for if God could work through Mary, he could equally work through, say, Joseph. In other words, belief in the incarnation is not necessarily dependent on a "miracle." Perhaps we should class the incarnation, like creation and redemption, as an event "outside nature," which is still more marvelous than a physical miracle. Like creation and redemption, the incarnation is a truth of monumental importance from a theological point of view; but it is not one that depends on any single "inexplicable" physical event. However, if miracles, in the strict sense of the term, are not essential to Christian belief (issues concerning the resurrection apart), then perhaps we should be less concerned with them.

The second reason liberals have backed away from an emphasis on miracles is that once a definition like Aquinas's is adopted, it is impossible to prove that a miracle has occurred. Here the basic argument has been given by David Hume (though he can be criticized for giving a very misleading definition of miracle).[68] However extraordinary an event appears to be, it is always possible, with ingenuity, to come up with an explanation that fits our worldview. For example, if I don't believe in ghosts, whatever experiences I have in that realm can be attributed to either fraud or unknown but natural phenomena, or (if I am desperate) the claim that I must have been hypnotized. Sometimes, moreover, it is perfectly legitimate to protect our established worldview via interpretations such as these, though there is clearly a danger of avoiding the challenges provided by genuinely new phenomena. However, the upshot is that while it may be perfectly rational for someone who already believes in God to think that occasionally there are miracles (in the strict sense of the term), someone who doesn't believe in God can never, by force of observation and logic, be forced to accept them as miracles. As Hume put it, "No human testimony can have such force as to prove a miracle, and make it a just foundation for any such [popular] system of religion."[69] Despite my many reservations about Hume's overall philosophy, I believe that in this matter he was essentially correct.

The third reason why liberals are nervous about using miracles as demonstrations of religious truth goes right back to the Gospels, where again and again Jesus charged people not to spread abroad the extraordinary events they had experienced (e.g., Mark 5:43; 9:9). It appears that he did not want people to come to him and to accept his message because of what they could receive physically, but because of the intrinsic truth and beauty of the message. "There shall be no sign but the sign of Jonah" (Matt. 16:4). We must remember that in this parable the people who heard Jonah only had the "sign" of his preaching; they did not witness, and probably did not know about, his being swallowed by the great fish.

68. Hume defines a miracle as a "violation" of a law of nature, and he defines a "law of nature" in terms of "constant conjunction." Logically speaking, therefore, if a miracle occurred, there would no longer be constant conjunction, therefore no law of nature, and therefore no miracle. Today, when we speak of laws of nature, we think more in terms of statistical probabilities, and thus Hume's definition is unhelpful.

69. Hume, *An Inquiry Concerning Human Understanding* (1748), ed. L. A. Selby-Bigge, 2nd ed. (Oxford: Clarendon Press, 1902), X, II.

Moreover, when the Jonah story is taken as typology for the resurrection, we must also remember that the resurrection appearances were only to those who already believed Jesus to be the Messiah, with the exception of Paul, who already fervently believed in God.

There are two major exceptions to Jesus' call not to spread abroad the marvelous events that accompanied his ministry. The first is the raising of Lazarus, "that they may believe that you sent me" (John 11:42). Perhaps this was a special case, or perhaps — as elsewhere in John's Gospel — we have something closer to a meditation on the meaning of Jesus' life than the kind of (more or less) historical account of it given in the synoptic Gospels. In any case, one of the principal themes of John's Gospel is that Jesus is the light of the world, and that those who are attracted to him are attracted as by light (e.g., John 3:21; 8:12). There is also the suggestion that believing in the "works" is a possible, but less satisfactory, way than believing in Jesus simply for what he is (John 10:38). The second major exception is when, shortly after some works of healing, Jesus tells the disciples of John the Baptist to tell him "the things you have seen and heard" (Luke 7:22). According to tradition, the presence of the coming Messiah would be signified by a series of events that echoed the work of the prophet Elijah, and it was necessary for John to be reassured.

The conclusions of this short examination of miracles in the life of Christianity are:

(1) If we use the word "miracle," we must be careful about which sense we have in mind. In the broad sense of "amazing events," there is no doubt that many miracles occur; but in the strict sense — following Aquinas's definition — the issue is more complex.

(2) It is a mistake to try to prove the faith by old or new miracles. This was not the way of Jesus, and though genuinely amazing events may quite properly shake people out of their complacency and lead to a reevaluation of life, this is not the same as attempting to find a logically or scientifically watertight "proof."

(3) If one does believe in God, and does try to live "in the Spirit," life may suddenly become full of unexpected and "marvelous" happenings, as in the Acts of the Apostles. William Temple used to say that when he prayed he found that "coincidences" kept happening. However, in

this context, it is hard to know how far the works of the Spirit are the natural result of living in harmony with God, self, and nature, and how far miracles, in the strict sense, are involved. Whatever the full truth may be in this matter, there is no doubt that the miracles described in the New Testament have huge symbolic importance, and they can be used by Christian teachers when they try to explain the significance of the life of Jesus.

(4) Not all liberals have exactly the same view of miracles. When the word is used in its strict sense, some believe that such events do occasionally happen (and, in all probability, that the resurrection was one of these). Others not only deny that miracles, in the strict sense, are a necessary part of Christian belief; they doubt whether God ever uses them. Instead, God is thought to be active within the world in more subtle ways, and extraordinary things happen when — as in the healing miracles of Jesus or the events within the book of Acts — people walk in tune with God. A book on liberal theology published in 1908 identifies "the rejection of the miraculous" (when a miracle is defined in terms of divine "intervention") as the hallmark of the liberal tradition. This discussion indicates how much that is an oversimplification of the issues.[70]

(5) Those liberals who do believe in miracles (in the strict sense) are likely to say something like this: "I do not believe that Jesus is the Son of God because of the miracles; rather, I believe in (some of) the miracles because I believe that Jesus is the Son of God." In my view, this is a perfectly rational position to hold.

IN THE FOREGOING DISCUSSION of miracles I have not dealt with the special case of the resurrection, which has a unique place in Christian teaching, a place where one might reasonably argue that there is a case in which any mainstream version of Christianity is committed to a miracle (in the strict sense of the term).

This is a complex subject that I have discussed at some length else-

70. H. Egerton, *Liberal Theology and the Ground of Faith* (London: Pitman and Sons, 1908), pp. 3, 47. The book, though written by a relatively conservative Christian, is sympathetic to some aspects of what it calls "Liberal Theology" as a form of "Humanism" that seeks "a place for liberty" (p. 33).

where.[71] I have written that it might be helpful for the Christian to think of the resurrection in the same way as Aquinas thinks of creation and redemption (and as I have suggested we could think of the incarnation): that is, as a theological truth that does not depend on any single event in the historical order of things. I do not mean that there were not "events" that are related to the resurrection, such as the appearance to Mary, the walk to Emmaus, the sight of an empty tomb, and so on. Rather, I mean that no one of these events, nor any combination of them, can encapsulate what Christians mean by the resurrection. In addition to a belief about an event, or events, that happened in the past, the resurrection has a kind of existential meaning in terms of how it has an impact on us. In a similar vein, in commenting on this doctrine, Rowan Williams has written: "The untidy character of the stories leaves the reader or listener with work to do. Whatever else this is, it isn't the account of an event happening just to someone in the past. . . . If you do meet him, there is an influx of some vision and energy that takes you beyond your normal frame of reference."[72]

This is a classic example of how it is easy for the casual reader to misunderstand what I am suggesting. Let me summarize my position with respect to the resurrection as follows: the resurrection is a special case. I do regard it as a central teaching for mainstream Christianity and as one that is linked with a whole history of powerful experiences in which individual Christians (and sometimes others) have felt the presence of Jesus, especially at moments of crisis, even if most such experiences (because they have happened after the ascension) are not, strictly speaking, "resurrection experiences." However, it is possible to understand the resurrection, not as an "event" within the order of nature, but as something — like creation, redemption, and incarnation — that is of a different nature from miracles (in the straightforward sense of the term). From this perspective, Christians may take a variety of positions about exactly what events occurred on and after Easter Sunday; but, at the same time, they may share a commitment to the truth of the resurrec-

71. See Langford, *Unblind Faith*, pp. 135-46.
72. Rowan Williams, "Easter — the Awkward Time of Year," *The Daily Telegraph*, News Review on Saturday, March 26, 2005, p. 21.

tion as a doctrine — concerning the presence of the living Christ — that has huge implications for the future of both our species and our individual selves.

Furthermore, Christians like me, who affirm a belief in the resurrection, are not always happy to refer to this as a *physical* resurrection because of ambiguities about what "physical" implies. If we accept the belief that the resurrection stories seek to describe genuine experiences of the first Christians, it is clear that whatever body the resurrected Jesus had was very different from the bodies we have here and now. However, there are two stories that imply something closely associated with what we usually mean by "physical," namely, the claim that the risen Jesus ate fish (Luke 24:42-43) and the account of Jesus' invitation to Thomas to feel his wounds (John 20:27). Just how these stories can be blended with an overall approach to the nature and meaning of the resurrection is a question that, quite frankly, still puzzles me. It is one of many situations where I am still exploring the full implications of seeking to be a disciple of Jesus.

CHAPTER THREE

Thirteen Key Figures in the Liberal Christian Tradition

———— ⊗⊗⊗ ————

A. Introduction

We have already seen that when people ask for the meaning of a word, sometimes an indication of a set of typical characteristics is more useful than a simple definition. Another way of approaching the meaning of many words is to see how they are used within a body of literature or discourse. For example, although one may try to define "God" as "the creative source of the universe," such a definition runs into many problems, even though it may form a useful starting point in some discussions. In particular, not all people, especially in the East, use the word "God" in this way; furthermore, words such as "creative" and "source" and "universe" are themselves problematic. An alternative approach is to see how the word is used, and undergoes subtle changes, within the Bible, or — for different religious traditions — within other bodies of holy writings, or — in nonliterate societies — within bodies of discourse and ritual. Such an approach can help us see what is common to different traditions (e.g., all those that use the word "God" point to some kind of "ultimate" force or explanation) and in what ways they differ.

In this chapter I am attempting to do much the same with the word "liberal" as it is used in the tradition of liberal theology, though on a much smaller scale. An understanding of what the tradition stands for can grow when we investigate how the tradition is exemplified in thirteen influential people. I will thus give some flesh and bone, as it were, to the eleven typical characteristics described in chapter 2. I must emphasize that not all those included here should be classed as liberals in the sense that the term has acquired in the twenty-first century. For example, if I were asked to say whether or not Justin Martyr should be classed as a "liberal" theologian in the sense in which that term is now likely to be used, the answer would certainly be no. However, he is significant because of at least one major contribution that he made to the building up of the tradition.[1]

(1) Justin Martyr

Justin, martyred in Rome in 165 CE, was one of the first Christian apologists whose writings — or at least some of whose writings — have survived. We have seen that the original meaning of "apology" is a defense, and Justin sought to commend the Christian faith to the pagan world by using rational arguments. As we would expect at this early date, not all of his views are shared by later liberals. For example, he held a belief in the importance of demons that now seems very strange; and one of his principal grounds for proving the Christian faith was the alleged fulfillment of prophecy. (Nowadays, prophecy is still seen as important, but more in the sense of the "forthtelling" of moral and spiritual truths than in the sense of "foretelling" the future.) As with many contemporary sects, Justin's claims that we can see the present, and even the distant future, being foretold within Scripture, especially in any detail, can

1. Only a few books have attempted to explain the liberal Christian tradition by this use of key exemplars. One that I have already referred to is John Tulloch's *Rational Theology and Christian Philosophy in the Seventeenth Century* (Edinburgh and London: Blackwood, 1872), 2 vols.; another is E. A. George, *Seventeenth Century Men of Latitude* (London: Fisher and Unwin, 1909), which includes Chillingworth, Smith, and Taylor (as I do in this volume), and adds John Hales, Benjamin Whichcote, Henry More, Sir Thomas Browne, and Richard Baxter. See also J. B. Mullinger, *The University of Cambridge* (Cambridge: Cambridge University Press, 1911), vol. 3, pp. 588-662, for vignettes of the Cambridge Platonists.

nearly always be seen as dependent on contrived and one-sided readings of a text.

Nevertheless, in many ways Justin typified a kind of rational Christianity that was to have enormous consequences. Instead of seeing the Bible and Greek philosophy as rivals, he saw them as companions, especially within the tradition of Socrates, one of the philosophers he called "a Christian before Christ." We can see that he read these Greek sources with a considerable degree of selection, but despite that fault, for many Christians he established a serious respect for reason, which he thought should be used alongside Scripture. In doing so, Justin took advantage of the claim in John's Gospel (1:14) that the *Logos* (which can be translated as either "word" or "reason") is made flesh in Jesus.

There are other important themes in Justin: a view of history, for example, that sees Jesus' Second Coming as the culmination of God's plan; a recognition that not all Christians believed in the virgin birth, though he himself did; the use of allegory in interpreting the Bible in order to harmonize it with reason; and belief in free will.[2] In addition, Justin was able to respect a source and criticize it at the same time. Thus, although he admired Plato, he disagreed with the idea that the human soul has a kind of eternity apart from God's grace; and while he admired the Stoics, he criticized their tendency toward pantheism.[3] Overall, despite his faults, Justin did a great service in beginning to see how reason can and should be used by Christians in order to both understand and spread their faith. It is interesting that Henry Bettenson, in his introduction to passages from Justin in his *Documents of the Christian Church,* refers to him as a "liberal" — as he does Clement of Alexandria.[4]

---

2. Justin Martyr, *Dialogue with Trypho,* trans. T. B. Falls (Washington, DC: The Catholic University of America Press, 1948), sec. 48.

3. Stoic language often sounds very like that of Christianity, but for classical Stoics, God is not "personal" in the sense of being aware of — let alone loving toward — every person. Our immortality arises when our individual egos are totally absorbed into the universal "Reason," as when a spark rejoins the fire from which it came. Similarly, some Eastern religions deny any lasting value to our individuality.

4. Henry Bettenson, *Documents of the Christian Church,* 2nd ed. (Oxford: Oxford University Press, 1963).

(2) Origen

By all accounts, Origen was one of the most brilliant minds in the ancient world. Born in Alexandria in about 185 CE, he spent most of his life teaching and writing in that city. His scholarly work covered Greek philosophy and Jewish thought in addition to the Bible. During the persecution of Christians under the Emperor Decius, he was tortured, and he died in about 254, probably as a result of his injuries. As with Justin, not all of his ideas were taken up by liberals, though the most controversial of his views is still attractive to some. This view, sometimes known as "universalism," is the suggestion that eventually all, including even the devil himself, will respond to the love of God and be saved. (However, there is a scholarly debate as to whether this was Origen's considered opinion at the end of his life.[5]) Another aspect of his thought that is not generally followed is his belief that the injustices of this world are, in part, a consequence of sins committed by us in a former life, a view that is close to the Hindu doctrine of karma. While there are some Christians who accept a reincarnational view, including many of the Cambridge Platonists, the majority, including most liberals, do not.[6] However, this matter illustrates Origen's attempt, like that of Justin, to push the possibility of a rational explanation as far as possible.

Closely related to this emphasis on reason is Origen's famous theory of biblical inspiration as requiring, according to the context, a blend of literal, moral, and spiritual (or allegorical) interpretation. Consider, for example, the proper way to use the book of Joshua, with its bloody account of the conquest of Canaan, sometimes with wholesale slaughters of children, all apparently sanctioned by God. Origen makes the follow-

5. When he did support universalism, he added the idea that following universal salvation there would then be another fall and another cycle of sin and redemption, and so on forever.

6. Christian versions of reincarnation include the proviso that, once a person is truly "in Christ," the cycle of lives is finished. One of the difficulties with this theory is that even though, under hypnosis, most people can produce a detailed account of alleged former lives, it is very hard to prove that these are not a product of the creative unconscious mind acting on information stored in the brain. Even if (and this is much disputed) genuinely new information is provided, once any paranormal activity is admitted, it is difficult to prove that the information came from a former life.

ing points: (1) the spiritual has priority over the literal meaning of a text; (2) a literal meaning is not always present; (3) passages like that describing the total destruction of Ai — when properly interpreted — refer to the conquest of human vices rather than the conquest of peoples; and (4) we should always interpret Scripture to promote "things worthy of God."[7]

These issues are still alive: many conservative Christians feel that they must believe that God ordered the terrible events recorded in Joshua and elsewhere because this is what Scripture says. They usually add, in a kind of defense, either that we are in no position to judge God or that the slaughter was an unfortunate necessity that can serve as no precedent for later times. For the liberal, both defenses are inadequate, and they seriously call into doubt the meaning of claims about God being good and just. (We might note here how recent attempts to defend incidences of ethnic cleansing also appeal to the alleged "special circumstances" of the situation.)

Another aspect of Origen's teaching that is important for the liberal tradition is his emphasis on human free will, along with his attempt to make this compatible with a comprehensive belief in providence (an issue discussed in the previous chapter). One of the ways he tries to deal with this can be found in an extended discussion of how to interpret the biblical claim that God hardened Pharaoh's heart, which appears to remove his free will and responsibility (e.g., Exod. 10:1). In this particular case, I do not find Origen's account of the "figurative" use of language convincing; but it does express an honest attempt to believe in both free will and some kind of divine Lordship over history.[8] (I prefer simply to say that this story reflects a primitive view in which every event had, in some sense, to reflect the will of God. This preceded more subtle accounts of what is meant by omnipotence and omniscience.)

---

7. Origen, *Homilies on Joshua*, trans. B. J. Bruce, ed. C. White (Washington, DC: The Catholic University of America Press, 2002), pp. 8, 85-94, 127-29, 189; Origen, *On First Principles*, trans. G. W. Butterworth (London: SPCK, 1936), pp. 277-78, 292.

8. Origen, *On First Principles*, chap. 1.

(3) Peter Abelard

Peter Abelard (1079-1142) is best known to the general public for his love affair with Heloise, and the infamous castration arranged by her uncle that followed his secret marriage to her. His lectures in Paris and his writings frequently got him into trouble with the authorities because they combined a healthy skepticism with an optimistic belief in the power of human reason that frequently led to unsettling questions. He was aware of the intolerance of the age, and one of his most important works, entitled *Sic et Non* ("Yes and No"), carefully describes the arguments for and against a series of opinions, and then leaves the matter there, without indicating what his own view is. In this way he was able to introduce reasoning and doubt into many controversial areas without committing himself to any heresy.

In addition to this major contribution to theological method, I shall single out four positions taken by Abelard that are of prime importance for the liberal tradition.

First is his rejection of original guilt. His position is not based on questioning the Vulgate's misleading translation of the Greek of Romans 5:12 (as a Latinist, Abelard may not have been aware of that) but on the moral and logical difficulties of being born "guilty," given his belief that a free act of intention to disobey the moral law must precede any meaningful "guilt" *(culpa)*. As a person of his time, he accepts that Adam, in the original creation, was immortal, and that we all suffer death because of his sin; but he insists that we inherit this consequence of his guilt (sometimes he refers, perhaps rather oddly, to receiving "punishment" for Adam's sin) but not the guilt itself, until — at an early age — we ourselves cooperate with evil.[9] Similarly, sin in general, and original sin in particular, are associated with human "weakness," in contrast to God's power.[10]

Second, and more influential, is Abelard's account of redemption,

9. Abelard, *Expositio in Epistolam ad Romanos,* Patrologia Latina (hereafter P.L.), vol. 178, ed. J-P. Migne, p. 866 (modern edition [Latin and German] ed. R. Peppermuller [Freiburg: Herder, 2000], p. 428); cf. D. E. Luscombe, *Peter Abelard's Ethics* (Oxford: Clarendon Press, 1971), pp. xxxiv-xxxv, 20-22, 56.

10. Abelard, *Christian Theology,* P.L., vol. 178, p. 1321.

often called the "exemplary theory of atonement." The loving example of Jesus, both in his life and death, is such that people can be *drawn* to repentance and a new vision of life in a way that would otherwise be impossible. Abelard describes how, when we are redeemed, we acquire true liberty for the first time because we can do what is right, not out of fear but solely out of our love for him who showed such love to us, a love that led Jesus to lay down his life for his friends.[11] Similarly, Jesus is reported as saying: "If I be lifted up from the earth, I will *draw* all men to me" (John 12:32).

Conservative Christians sometimes complain that this "exemplary theory" is only "subjective," that is, instead of emphasizing a cosmic victory that Jesus won on the cross, it merely emphasizes the psychological power of the example of a good man. However, this objection seriously underrates the power of Abelard's argument, in my view. It is true that any example of loving sacrifice can draw us to respond; but the cross, for the Christian, is not just any example. If Jesus is indeed the *Logos* of God, then here is a *cosmic* statement. Love, which so many people — religious and nonreligious alike — recognize as being the most important element in human experience, is shown to be the ultimate meaning of life. Of course, unless one believes in a loving God, the full significance of this cosmic event will be missed, for it will be just another example of a beautiful and perhaps awe-inspiring act. But for the believer, since it is God's Messiah or image that is demonstrating this love, the real nature of God is revealed. Here we have a prime example of what I have called revelation, something that is not against reason (except in the sense of contradicting our ordinary expectations) but that goes beyond reason (a distinction strongly endorsed by Aquinas). It is a disclosure by God, in this case in and through both a person and an event.

In this situation the language of discovery is appropriate, just as it is in science when a new insight, such as that of Copernicus or Newton, enables us to see things in a new way. Here the discovery is about the significance of love. For the believer, love is not only something we choose to value, nor even something that we find helps to make the world a better and happier place (which is a kind of "discovery," albeit with a small *d*, as it

---

11. Abelard, *Expositio in Epistolam ad Romanos*, P.L., vol. 178, p. 836.

were). It is a Discovery about what the world was created for, and about what gives ultimate meaning to human life. Love is not only a powerful psychological force (though it is that), but is also a truth about the universe. It is difficult to make sense of such language unless one believes that we live in a universe that is the creation of a loving intelligence.

Seen in this way, Jesus' life and death take on a whole new dimension. Here are both events within history and unique symbols in which, once and for all, God demonstrates that he is prepared to identify himself with the human condition, accepting the vulnerability of being first a baby and then a mortal man in order to share our lives, refusing to accept angelic help when the going gets rough. Like the Good Samaritan, Jesus travels alongside the one in need. I do not claim that Abelard's theory tells us the whole truth about the redemption or atonement (nor did Abelard himself make such a claim); but I do suggest that it is part of any adequate explanation, and that it is not purely "subjective." A symbolic act of this kind, as I have intimated, acquires a cosmic, and "objective," significance and power.

Third, Abelard's approach to the Bible echoes Origen's. While never denying the literal truth of any part of Scripture, he insists that if a passage strikes us as absurd, we should suspect that either the translation is faulty or that we have not grasped the true meaning of it.[12]

Fourth, in contrast to most of his contemporaries, he argued that heretics should be presented with reasoning rather than force.[13]

(4) Sebastian Castellio

Castellio, a scholar of Latin, Greek, and Hebrew, was born in Savoy in 1515 (in French he was called Châteillon). In 1540, while studying at Lyons, he witnessed the Inquisition's execution by burning of three Lutherans, and that apparently precipitated his conversion to Protestantism. Fleeing from the Inquisition, he became a schoolmaster in Geneva, where he began one of several translations of the Bible. Although he was for a time a

12. Abelard, prologue to *Sic et Non*, P.L., vol. 178, p. 1347.
13. Abelard, *Intr. Ad Theologiam*, P.L., vol. 178, p. 1048.

friend of Calvin, his criticisms of the Geneva clergy, not only for intolerance but also for impurity and drunkenness, along with his rejection of some of Calvin's teachings, led to his banishment from Geneva in 1544, following complaints from Calvin himself. There followed years of poverty in which he supported his large family by doing menial work by day and working nights on his translations. Then, in 1553, he was appointed professor of Greek at Basel in recognition of his scholarly work. The following year, largely in reaction to the burning death of Servetus in Geneva (in 1553), he and his friend Caelius Curio published his most famous work, *Concerning Heretics and Whether They Should Be Persecuted (De haereticis, an sint persequendi)*. Curio provided an anthology of Christian appeals for toleration, some from early church fathers, others from more recent writers, including Erasmus. Castellio provided the argument via prefaces and other contributions under a number of assumed names.

We find here the first substantial Christian defense of toleration since the time when the churches gained political power. It provoked significant reaction from the established churches and has become a classic. Prior to the Reformation era, Christian appeals for toleration either date from the time when the church was itself a persecuted minority, or represent rare dissenting voices.[14] Moreover, the reasoning behind Castellio's thinking is surprisingly relevant to our day. Not only does he point out the extraordinary contrast between the character of Jesus and that of the persecutors; he insists that we have no right to be intellectually certain in the matters about which people are being burned alive. Here the theme of liberal rationality is especially evident, for he does not dismiss faith, but he recognizes our inability to *know* some things in a way that foreshadows much Enlightenment thinking. The difference is that Castellio couples this acceptance of doubt with an appreciation of the real possibility of faith — in something that goes beyond our full comprehension. Here, I hold, Castellio is actually more rational than typical followers of the Enlightenment, who tend to exaggerate the power of human reason and (unreasonably) rule out the possibility of revelation.

14. In the Reformation era, Castellio had a few forerunners, most notably the Anabaptist Balthasar Hubmaier, who was writing in the 1520s.

This point is underscored in Castellio's other important work, *The Art of Doubting*, published in 1563, just before his death.[15] As I emphasized in chapter 1, for liberal Christians the opposite of faith is not doubt, but faithlessness, while doubt is a legitimate — and indeed necessary — element in any serious rational inquiry. In *The Art of Doubting*, not only does Castellio argue this point, he also makes a significant contribution to what would later become the debate on biblical fundamentalism, particularly the belief that the Bible, in its original form, is verbally inspired. The liberal view is that the Bible is indeed "inspired," but that does not mean that all the words that appear in Scripture are literally God's words; many of them (and for some liberals, all of them) are human attempts to express a divine vision in human words. As we have seen, some early writers, notably Origen, emphasized the nonliteral use of Scripture; but even in Origen there is an implicit belief that the original text is not a human creation. The more modern view, that Scripture is inspired but not verbally inspired, only becomes explicit in some sixteenth- and seventeenth-century Christians, including Castellio. In his *The Art of Doubting* he thus compares biblical language to that of an ambassador who is sent with a message to another king. The ambassador begins by repeating some actual words that he has been told to say, but then, as he is required to expand on the message, he begins to use his own words.[16] Similarly, Castellio is suggesting, some of the biblical writers' words may be actually dictated by God, but many others are attempts to express a message in their own words. Here we find a move away from a universal doctrine of verbal inspiration that enables us to make much more sense of many biblical passages and that also enables us to distance God from some of the cruelties that a literalist is almost bound to attribute to him.

Among the many other views of Castellio, one of the undersung

15. The full title is *De arte dubitandi et confidendi ignorandi et sciendi* (modern edition ed. E. F. Hirsch [Leiden: Brill, 1981]). The title is difficult to translate in a way that accurately expresses the sense of the terms in 1563, but goes something like this: "Concerning the art of doubting and of trusting, of being ignorant and of knowing." There is no English translation of the whole work, though sections are given in R. H. Bainton's translation of *De haereticis* (New York: Columbia University Press, 1935); but there is a French translation by C. Baudouin (Geneva: Jeheber, 1953).

16. Castellio, *The Art of Doubting*, I, chap. 15.

heroes of the Christian tradition, I shall mention just one, namely, his insistence that Christians should concentrate on a few "core," or essential, doctrines and leave the rest to legitimate personal choice. Here his view echoes that of the Roman Catholic Erasmus, who wrote: "We define so many things which may be left in ignorance or in doubt without loss of salvation. . . . That which is forced cannot be sincere, and that which is not voluntary cannot please Christ."[17]

(5) Elizabeth I

Although it would be highly misleading to say that Elizabeth I was a "liberal" in the modern sense, I have decided to include her in this list because the debt that liberal Anglicanism owes her is not often appreciated. In 1558, when she ascended the throne, some three hundred Protestants had just been burned alive by the former Catholic regime, including many of the leaders who had not escaped to the Continent; naturally enough, there was a concern that there might be an equivalent bloodbath as Protestants took their revenge. The situation was complicated by the fact that, while Catholics of the time considered Protestants "heretics," for whom the death penalty had been established for many centuries, Protestants did not normally use the word "heresy" to refer to Catholic belief.[18] (During the reign of Elizabeth, heresy was defined in such a way that all those who believed in the Trinity and the incarnation were effectively safe from that charge.[19]) Nevertheless, many Protestants did want revenge, and not only were some of them just as intolerant as their Catholic counterparts had been, but all who failed to take the oath recognizing Elizabeth as supreme governor of the church could be in danger of the charge of sedition. What happened is often seen as surpris-

17. Quoted in R. H. Bainton, *Erasmus of Christendom* (Tring, UK: Lion, 1969), pp. 224-25 (*Erasmi Epistolae,* Jan. 5, 1523).

18. On occasion, Luther called the pope a "heretic," but he was defining heresy in terms of not having true faith. See *Luther's Works* (Philadelphia: Fortress Press, 1967), 39:67; 54:41.

19. See P. Hughes, *A Popular History of the Reformation* (London: Hollis and Carter, 1957), p. 303.

ing, and, according to David Starkey, an indication of Elizabeth's "moderation" and "fundamental humanity." No one was burned at the stake; many were retired to their estates on the condition that they stay out of politics; those who refused were placed under arrest, but for the most part in surprisingly benign conditions. For example, Tunstal, Bishop of Durham, though confined to quarters, became a houseguest at Lambeth Palace.[20]

As is well known, some extreme cruelties were meted out to Catholic missionaries later in Elizabeth's reign.[21] However, the fundamental issue here was political rather than purely religious. Following the papal excommunication of Elizabeth in 1570, the Catholic missionaries were seen as — and often were — political as well as religious agents who argued that Mary Queen of Scots, and later the king of Spain, were the legitimate rulers of England. Needless to say, this was unacceptable to the ordinary Englishman, even before the defeat of the Spanish Armada in 1588. It must also be admitted that during Elizabeth's reign there were rare cases of execution for heresy in Norwich, such as the case of Francis Kett in 1589.[22]

Another matter that points to Elizabeth's moderation is her approach to the Roman Catholic doctrine of transubstantiation, namely, the claim that during Holy Communion the bread and wine are changed into the "substance" of the body and blood of Christ.[23] Some background is needed before we come to Elizabeth's famous response. The vast majority of Protestants refused to accept transubstantiation, though their reasons varied. At one extreme were those, like Zwingli, who said that

20. David Starkey, *Elizabeth: Apprenticeship* (London: Vintage, 2001), pp. 302-6.

21. Particularly tragic was the fate of Thomas Campion, who proclaimed a Catholic faith but did not want to dethrone Elizabeth.

22. I am aware of only three other executions for heresy in Elizabeth's long reign: Matthew Hamont in 1579, John Lewes in 1583, and Peter Cole in 1587. All four executions were in Norwich, where there seem to have been at least two persecuting bishops.

23. In the official Catholic teaching, "accidents," such as taste, remain those of bread and wine, while the "substance" is changed. Part of the difficulty here is that not everyone uses the notions of substance and accident in the same way. Consequently, despite the bitter history of the debate, I am one of those liberals who holds that the Catholic-Protestant debate has been riddled with misunderstandings, and I am not convinced that, properly assessed, this is one of the topics on which there need be significant disagreement.

Holy Communion was only a "memorial" of what happened at the Last Supper; others, including most Anglicans, said that this was insufficient to explain the importance of the action. According to both Luther and Calvin, though the Catholic doctrine of transubstantiation should be rejected, Holy Communion was not only an act of remembrance but also a divinely ordained means of grace. In the context of the competing theories, one view that has become typical of the liberal tradition goes like this: "Although, strictly speaking, Christ's sacrifice is not 'reenacted' — because it happened 'once for all' at Calvary — Holy Communion is nonetheless both a powerful symbol and a God-given sacrament, in which, through the taking of the bread and wine, we are given God's grace in a special way. When we celebrate the Lord's Supper, we enter into the spirit of a timeless event by means of an act of empathy and imagination. Here is much more than a 'memorial.' It is not so much a reenactment, however, as a 'reentry.' As to the exact nature of the bread and the wine received, it is wise not to be too specific, but in a powerful, symbolic sense, it is the body and blood of Christ. Beyond that, it is best to be silent."[24]

The story goes that, while the priests came to question Elizabeth during the reign of her half sister, the Catholic Queen Mary, when it came to the doctrine of transubstantiation, she refused either to assent or to reject the doctrine. Instead, she responded with a short verse:

'Twas Christ the Word that spake it.
The same took bread and brake it,
And as the Word did make it,
So I believe and take it.[25]

This provides a very powerful example of the "liberal" approach, which fully accepts the power of many symbolic actions, while seeing no need to provide a precise definition of what is happening that should be binding on all.

24. The words are mine, but I believe they typify the via media.
25. The verse has come down to us in several similar versions. That it was literally part of Elizabeth's reply cannot be proved; but not only is it possible — it fits well with what is known about Elizabeth's views and wit.

(6) Richard Hooker

Richard Hooker (1554-1600) spent much of his early life as an Oxford don. Following his marriage, he had a short spell as Master of the Temple and then accepted a country living in order to live quietly and concentrate on his writing. The resulting collection of books, known collectively as *Of the Laws of Ecclesiastical Polity* (published between 1593 and 1662), has had an extraordinary following and indicates how a peace-loving scholar, who had little fame in his time, can have a huge influence after his death. Of the many streams within his thought, I shall indicate just three: (1) his "moderation," (2) his use of reason, and (3) his view of "certainty."

(1) Hooker represents a classic case of the via media, or middle way. He found England torn between two rival versions of Christianity, one represented by Roman Catholicism, united on many issues with some Anglicans, and the other by a narrow form of Presbyterianism that had a particular attachment to Calvin. His compromise and famous "moderation" was rooted in his approach to the Bible. He sided with the Calvinists and against the Catholicism of his time by accepting not only that the Bible was the supreme authority for Christians but also that nothing should be taught as necessary for salvation (or as an "article of faith") that was not based on it. However, he disagreed with the Calvinists of his day about their claim that all teachings (e.g., those concerning how the church should be governed in England) could be found in the Bible. For many such matters — because the Bible was silent — one had to accept what was "reasonable."

(2) His interpretation of the Bible was linked to a view of rationality that was much closer to that of Aquinas than to that of Calvin. This can be seen most clearly in the first book of his great work where, in magnificent Elizabethan prose, he sets out his view of the universal system of laws that explain the nature and scope of "natural law," which governs the role of human reason.

(3) Hooker's teaching on certainty is related to both his teaching on rationality and his moderation, in the latter case because it was a response to the Protestant doctrine of "assurance," which is still powerful in our day. That doctrine goes something like this: If we are of God's elect, it is vital to *know* that we are of this body, because otherwise there will be

such a constant anxiety that we might be destined for hell that Christian joy will be impossible. While Hooker did not accept the Calvinist account of predestination and election, he did have sympathy for those who continually worried about their status. Peace of mind makes up part of the good life, even though there may have to be occasions when it is disturbed. His solution was to contrast what he called "Certainty of Evidence," which we do *not* have in matters of faith (unlike the angels, who have "the light of glory"), and "Certainty of Adherence," which, by grace, we may have in spiritual matters. The latter relates to conviction rather than to intellectual certainty, and it is regarding this kind of certainty that Hooker describes how "the heart doth cleave and stick unto that which it doth believe."[26] The probable origin of the distinction can be found in Aquinas's *De Veritate (The Disputed Questions of Truth).*[27] Hooker's rejection of "certainty of evidence" echoes Castellio's "art of doubting" (though he arrived at it independently) and can be developed in a way that makes possible an appropriate sense of assurance that the religious person may come to have, and, at the same time, a denial that religious conviction can give one either a justified, philosophically certain starting point or a legitimate ground for forcing a belief on others.

Hooker's acceptance of uncertainty within recognizable forms of Christianity is especially relevant to contemporary thought. In his support of secular humanism and his rejection of Christianity (and all other forms of revealed religion), the scientist Hermann Bondi rooted his objections in the "supposed absolute certainty" of revealed religion.[28] This, however, is an argument from caricature. As I emphasized in chapter 1, just as I must judge atheistic philosophies by their best examples (for example, by admitting that the murderous actions of Lenin, Stalin, and

26. Richard Hooker, *Works,* 3rd edition, ed. J. Keble (Oxford: Oxford University Press, 1845), 3:470-71 (from a sermon dating from about 1585); cf. William Chillingworth, *The Religion of Protestants* (Oxford, 1638), 1, 9, p. 17, where the same terminology is used.

27. Aquinas, *De Veritate (The Disputed Questions of Truth),* trans. R. W. Mulligan (Chicago: Regnery, 1952), Q. 14, A. 1 *ad* 7.

28. This wording appears in Bondi's article "Arrogance of Certainty," available on the Internet but without publication details. Bondi expresses an equivalent view in his 1992 Conway Memorial Lecture (no. 67), "Humanism — the Only Valid Foundation of Ethics," published by the South Place Ethical Society.

many others, though committed in the name of an atheist philosophy, are irrelevant to a proper evaluation of atheism), so a fair-minded atheist or agnostic must consider the best examples of Christianity and not the Catholic Inquisition or the Calvinists' burning of Michael Servetus at the stake in Geneva. Such considerations might form part of a justifiable critique of both Catholic and Protestant institutions, but not of theism (including Christianity) itself. Here one might also point to the relevance of the old saw *corruptio optimi pessima* ("the corruption of the best is the worst"). For if Christianity, in its proper essence, represents a noble truth, one might well expect its distortions to be not better than atheism, but worse. To return to the theme of certainty, both Castellio and Hooker, though perhaps rare voices in their eras, were forerunners of a strongly held version of a contemporary liberal Christianity (a form of "revealed religion") that rejects absolute certainty as strongly as did Bondi.

(7) William Chillingworth

William Chillingworth (1602-1644) is included here as a representative of the "Great Tew Circle," a group of poets, philosophers, and theologians who met frequently at the home of Lord Falkland in the manor house at Great Tew, near Oxford, in the years leading up to the civil war. The group included some of the most brilliant men of the age, such as Ben Jonson and John Selden, in addition to Chillingworth. Thomas Hobbes was also a member for a short time, though most of his views were in no way typical of the group. Vignettes by some other members of this group, including Lord Falkland himself (Lucius Cary) and John Hales of Eton, could have served as representative of this circle of friends.

We have already come across Chillingworth in connection with the remarkable episode when, on his deathbed, he refused to recant his belief that those who held different beliefs could be saved provided they "endeavored" to pursue the good, as they saw it. The steps that led him to that conclusion can be related to key stages in his life.

One of the brightest stars of his generation at Oxford, Chillingworth, a poet, mathematician, philosopher, and theologian, became a fellow of

Trinity College in 1628. Shortly afterward, to the consternation of his many friends and admirers, he converted to Roman Catholicism and set off for the Jesuit training college at Douay. His principal reason, recorded in his letters, was his inability to answer the claim that, if humans were to be saved, God must have left an infallible source of necessary truth, and only the Roman Catholic Church sufficed to provide this. Within a few months, however, the experience of Douay convinced him of his mistake, and he returned to Anglicanism. His most famous work, *The Religion of Protestants,* published late in 1637, contains his carefully considered answer to the very question that had led to his conversion to Catholicism. He accepted the premise that God must have left, in this world, sufficient signs for those who wished to know the path to salvation; but this path was to be found, he insisted, within the Bible, along with sufficient human reason to interpret it. "The Scripture, we pretend, in things necessary is plain and perfect."[29] This, in turn, led to a typical liberal emphasis on a few fundamental teachings that were central to Christianity, teachings that he believed to be contained in the Apostles' Creed.

Notwithstanding my admiration for Chillingworth, this position — which typifies that of many liberal Christians — contains two problems that have not always been adequately faced. First, there is the need to show that it is the Christian Bible, and not some other body of Scripture, that should be the focus of attention. Second, even when the Bible is the accepted focus, not all intelligent readers of the Bible have come to the conclusion that the whole content of the Apostles' Creed is thereby proved, especially those within the Unitarian traditions.

I shall not pursue the first problem here except to point out that Chillingworth's position is moderated by his insistence that error does not necessarily lead to damnation, and by his more general teaching on "endeavor."[30] Furthermore, his book was addressed to a readership in Christian Europe, not a world community that included Buddhists, Muslims, and members of the other great world religions. With respect to the second point, I must note that the Apostles' Creed is not anywhere near

29. William Chillingworth, *The Religion of Protestants,* 2, 11, p. 57.
30. Chillingworth, *The Religion of Protestants,* 2, 160, p. 117.

as explicitly Trinitarian as the other principal creeds of the Christian faith, the Nicene and the Athanasian. In point of fact, Chillingworth strongly objected to the Athanasian Creed, largely because of its "anathemas," that is, its condemning to damnation those who would not agree with it.[31] The Apostles' Creed does refer to Jesus as God's "only Son, our Lord," but the nature of this sonship is left undefined, unlike the language of the other creeds, and for this reason a broad range of Christians have felt willing to embrace it. Nevertheless, my own view is that contemporary Christian liberals should admit that an acceptance of even a toned-down Trinitarianism is "going beyond" what is "plainly revealed" in the Bible. (Elsewhere, I have defended this going beyond as at least a plausible option and at best an exciting possibility that opens up new vistas.[32] I will revisit the relationship of the Trinity to the liberal tradition in chapter 4 below.)

Other indications of Chillingworth's contribution to the liberal tradition are worth bringing out. One is his dislike of what he called "blind zeal."[33] Here, as with his mentor, Richard Hooker, he is referring to the polemical nature of the rivalry between hard-line Calvinists on the one side and traditionalist Roman Catholics on the other, a rivalry that is still to be found in the debate between some "Catholics" and "evangelicals," though the fanatics of both persuasions do injustice to the terms. (The original sense of *catholic* comes from the Greek for "universal" [church], while that of *evangelical* comes from the word for "good news." If understood in their proper senses, liberals should claim to be both.) In this regard, it is interesting to find Chillingworth quoting Hooker's exact expression of the difference between "Certainty of Evidence" (which we do

31. See P. Des Maizeaux, *An Historical and Critical Account of the Life and Writings of Wm Chillingworth* (London, 1725), p. 81. The controversy over the use of the Athanasian Creed resurfaced many times, notably in the London weekly *The Guardian* of 1872 (vol. 27, esp. April 17, p. 503), where we find Tait, the Archbishop of Canterbury, and Frederick Temple (then the bishop of Exeter) among those who, while accepting its positive teaching, question its public use, especially in light of the anathemas.

32. Michael J. Langford, *A Liberal Theology for the Twenty-First Century: A Passion for Reason* (Aldershot, UK: Ashgate, 2001), chap. 7; see also Langford, *Unblind Faith*, 2nd ed. (Tunbridge Wells, UK: Parapress, 2010), chap. 6, and the section on the doctrine of the Trinity in chap. 4 below.

33. Des Maizeaux, *Life and Writings of Wm Chillingworth*, pp. 32-33.

not have) and "Certainty of Adherence" (which we can acquire).[34] Further, when he speaks of a "tyrannical God" who condemns those who make honest mistakes, a view of God he finds on both sides of the polemical debate, he adds this comment: "I for my part fear I should not love God, if I should think so strangely of him."[35] Congruently, in his defense of toleration, he condemns the use of violence and of "Machiavillian [*sic*] police" in order to make people conform in matters of religion, which can so easily "make men counterfeit."[36] Yet another indication of Chillingworth's liberal views was his initial refusal to accept the Thirty-nine Articles of Religion, legally in force since 1571, even though this delayed his preferment.[37] This is also a matter that liberal Christians who are members of the Church of England often feel urgently needs reform, with a complete rethinking of what Articles of Faith should be mandated for the clergy.

Chillingworth's claim that the one thing needful for salvation is to "endeavor" to do the good, as one sees it, while attractive, raises a difficulty that requires some comment. This claim, like that of Kant when he claims that the only thing good without qualification is "the good will," can appear to approve suicide bombers or other fanatics, provided only that — however mistaken — (1) they genuinely believe that they are doing the right thing, *and* (2) that their motive is simply and entirely to do the right thing (and not, for example, intended to secure a reward in heaven). Quite apart from any evaluation of what I call liberal theology, this is a serious issue in moral philosophy. My own view (which involves a criticism that Chillingworth's claim can only be supported within a wider discussion concerning the nature of the good) is that, in addition to the demand to endeavor to follow the good, we also have a responsibility to develop

34. Chillingworth, *The Religion of Protestants*, 1, 9, p. 37 and 2, 154, pp. 112-114.
35. Chillingworth, *The Religion of Protestants*, 2, 104, p. 92.
36. Chillingworth, *The Religion of Protestants*, 5, 96, p. 297.
37. Later in life, Chillingworth subscribed to the Articles, insisting on his acceptance of the general doctrine contained in them rather than in all of their individual teachings, and in consequence he received the chancellorship of Sarum. In recent decades many people have been ordained within the Church of England on the understanding that the assent to the Articles is a general one, rather than an explicit approval of every sentence. It is interesting to find that this "fudging" has its roots in the seventeenth century and is not just a recent way of getting around the difficulties.

some coherent notion of what the good is. This is partly to be found, I suggest, via Aristotle's emphasis on the need to acquire genuine virtue through how we manage our whole lives, which will hugely affect how we see "the good," and partly by emphasizing Aristotle's claim that we have the potential to respond to the "eye for the good," with which the virtuous person is endowed by nature (*Nichomachean Ethics,* 1114a-b).

I fully support Chillingworth's claim that it makes no moral sense to think that God will condemn sincere followers of other "ways" (or *dao*); but it does not follow that the right intention, or endeavor — especially in the long term — is the only thing that is necessary. Furthermore, the kinds of people Chillingworth has in mind are typical examples of "good" Muslims and Jews (and, I would add, secular humanists) who follow the Golden Rule and are as likely to be horrified by the actions of suicide bombers as are liberal Christians. The situation is paralleled by the distinction between conscience — when used to refer simply to a momentary feeling — and the kind of developed "conscience" described in Bishop Butler's account of reflecting in "a cool hour," and also by the medieval distinction between *conscientia* and *synderesis.*

(8) John Smith

John Smith (ca. 1616-1652) was a member of the important group of philosophers and theologians known as the Cambridge Platonists. I could have selected several of these for inclusion in this list of thirteen key figures, but I use Smith here — as I did in the case of Chillingworth and the Great Tew Circle — as a representative of that group. His *Select Discourses,* published posthumously in 1660, contain a number of themes that were typical of the latitudinarian tradition of which he was a part, and I shall limit myself to four of those that have special importance in our own time.

First, as with all the Cambridge Platonists, Smith emphasizes the importance of reason or rationality in the Christian life; but in his case he makes a useful attempt to describe the nature of reason in a way that explores how feelings and intuitions are related to overall rationality. Here we must tread carefully, because the extreme position — namely, that only "good" people (with the right feelings and intuitions) are capable of reason — is clearly untenable, since no matter how we define "badness," there is no doubt that some bad people are clever and can have at least a kind of rationality to a very high degree. However, Smith does not identify rationality with goodness. To appreciate what he is getting at, we may note his approval of Aristotle's claim that politics should not be taught to the young because they do not have the necessary experiential knowledge of human character in the world of human relationships. It is possible that he draws too strong a conclusion from this argument, as, for example, when he says that some people's hearts are too bad to have good heads. It is both silly and patronizing to counter an atheist's argument by saying that they need to grow spiritually in order to see the force of a religious argument. Nevertheless, it is true that our rational faculty does not work in isolation from both our experience and our whole character, especially in the more creative or imaginative aspects of reason. This interconnection of reason with character and sensibility is particularly evident, for example, when we try to see patterns or new possibilities or make judgments, and when there is no single and obviously true and simple answer. This complexity is one of the reasons why rational argument concerning questions of religion is so difficult and controversial — both in the past and the present.

Second, Smith's account of reason is linked with his rejection of both atheism and superstition in interesting ways. It is superstition that pictures God as an angry being who delights in hellfire and who combines an unhealthy "composition of fear and flattery."[38] Superstition is directly linked, in turn, with his account of atheism, which often arises because "a base opinion of the Deity as cruel and tyrannical" provokes negation and defiance when met by "more stout and surly natures" (p. 42). The odd mixture of "stout" and "surly" succeeds in expressing both Smith's sympathy for and rejection of atheism, though the term "surly" is, in my view, unfair. However, Smith's main point is exceedingly powerful and perhaps better expressed when he says, "Atheism could never have so easily crept into the world, had not Superstition made way and opened a

---

38. Smith, *Select Discourses* (London, 1669), p. 33. Hereafter, specific page references to this work appear in parentheses in the text.

back door for it" (p. 42). When I argue with atheist friends, I often conclude that they have (rightly) rejected a caricature of God, or of the Christian tradition, and that if only theism in general and Christianity in particular could be presented at their best they would receive much more
sympathetic treatment. This does not apply to all those who call themselves atheists, but a surprising number of them do reject a caricature.

Third, Smith is a typical exponent of the Anglican via media. For example, when he comes to the question of "justification by faith," he expresses the absolute need of both God's grace and of a genuinely re-
formed life. Commenting on those who do not realize how superstition
has entered into their own Christian faith, he refers to those who, "laying
aside all sober and serious care of true piety, think it sufficient to offer up
their saviour, his active and passive righteousness, to a severe and rigid
justice, to make expiation of those sins they can be willing to allow themselves in" (p. 37). This passage, expressed in the rather ponderous-
sounding style of the seventeenth century, should not be seen as a denial
of "justification by faith" but as a wise warning to those who oversimplify
it, and also, I suggest, as a warning to those who think of the atonement
in terms of the substitution theory. When justification is properly understood, it has to involve a change in human nature and not only a pardon-
ing and remitting of sins; otherwise, it is only what Smith calls a "name"
(p. 329).

Smith's account of justification is closely linked with a contrast between the inwardness of genuine faith and the externality of bad religion.
At times he falls into the mistake, common to many Christian apologists,
of making a sharp division between Pharisaism, with its emphasis on external obedience to the law, and the gospel, with its emphasis on inner
love. It is now widely recognized that, although the emphasis on exter-
nals did indeed characterize some Pharisees, it is simply unfair so to
characterize all of them; indeed, much in the Old Testament (e.g., in the
Psalms) only makes sense when we appreciate the internal side of faith.
Fortunately, Smith does not take an extreme position here, acknowledging that some Jews held true, internal faith in mercy and grace. Following Justin, he sees such people as "Christians" before their time (p. 323).
(As I have already indicated, I think it is misleading to call such people
"Christians," because it is better to restrict this term to those who articu-

late the belief that Jesus is the Christ.) Also, Smith condemns many Christians for reverting to a purely external version of obedience to Christ.

Fourth, there is Smith's forthright rejection of verbal inspiration. As I previously emphasized, all Christians, liberals included, agree that the Bible is "inspired"; but when it comes to explaining the nature of this inspiration, there is much disagreement. This is partly due to extreme difficulties when those holding this view encounter an allegedly loving God demanding the slaughter of innocents in the book of Joshua and elsewhere. The more conservative view is that the original text is verbally inspired by God: this means that every word was, as it were, dictated to the writer and is thus infallible. (This is the most general view of the nature of the Qur'an within Islam, though other views are now beginning to emerge.) John Smith, echoing some of the ideas of Sebastian Castellio, strongly disagrees: he claims that God typically works through human beings in a way that respects their freedom and allows for their own fallible interpretation of what they experience in some kind of vision. He supports his nonverbal account of revelation with references to earlier rabbinical accounts of inspiration, references made possible by his own scholarly knowledge of Hebrew and of rabbinic traditions. The higher forms of prophecy, he claims, make use of the human intellect, and further, "it seems most agreeable" to the nature of prophecy that "those words and phrases" in which the visions were expressed "should be the prophets' own" (pp. 180, 273).[39]

(9) Jeremy Taylor

Jeremy Taylor (1613-1667), the son of a barber, began his academic life at Cambridge as a sizar (a scholar needing financial assistance) at Gonville and Caius. He moved to Oxford, where, through the influence of William Laud — who was much impressed with his scholarship, even though Taylor did not share many of Laud's conservative opinions — he became

---

39. Smith was the dean of Queens' College, Cambridge, and was a Hebrew scholar, which enabled him to benefit from little-known rabbinic sources.

a fellow at All Souls College. Like Chillingworth, he then got tangled up in the civil war, as a result of which he was deprived of his living and spent at least two periods in prison at the hands of the Parliamentarians. Until the Restoration of 1660, he lived in difficult financial circumstances, spending some time as a schoolmaster. However, he continued to publish and eventually settled in Ireland, where he died as Bishop of Down and Connor in 1667.

Taylor has been most remembered for his devotional books, including the much-read *Holy Living* and *Holy Dying*. Although he was rightly respected as a person of spiritual insight as well as personal gentleness, his more pastoral works are not our concern here — except for his unconventional views on marriage. In two sermons entitled "The Marriage Ring," he argues against the long-held Augustinian tradition that sees human sexuality as something necessary for procreation but filled with a dangerous "lust" that needs to be avoided. In contrast to this view, Taylor advances a view of marriage that was far ahead of his time. For example, in addition to insisting that a wife should be a friend,[40] in his exposition of Genesis he writes: "[Adam] says not 'The woman which thou gavest *to* me' . . . but 'the woman thou gavest to be with me,' that is, to be my partner . . . not for dominion" (5:265, italics in original). Further, reflecting on the physical side of marriage, he says, "When a man dwells in love, then the breasts of his wife are pleasant as the droppings upon the little hill of Hermon . . ." (5:269). He returns to this theme in his *Discourse of the Nature, Offices, and Measures of Friendship,* where, during a discussion of all the different kinds of friendship, marriage is the "queen of friendship," and husband and wife are "best friends" (11:325). It is likely that his positive view of marriage reflects the two happy marriages of his own life.

His most important work, from the point of view of this essay, is certainly the *Liberty of Prophesying,* some of which may have been written while he was in prison as a result of the very intolerance he was attacking. "Prophesying," it should be said, had a much broader meaning in the seventeenth century than it does now: it referred primarily to the interpretation of Scripture, not to looking into the future. In many ways the

40. Jeremy Taylor, *Whole Works,* 15 vols., ed. R. Heber (London, 1828), 5:252. Hereafter, specific page references to this work appear in parentheses in the text.

argument follows Chillingworth's, but he specifically calls for the legal toleration of both Roman Catholics and Anabaptists, the two groups of Christians whom the contemporary Puritans most strongly opposed. Taylor's argument includes a historical account of the relative tolerance of the early church and the way in which the practice of persecution crept into it. He distinguishes sharply between the early practice of excommunication and the later practice of popes and bishops persuading emperors to punish heretics with fines, imprisonment, and death (8:137).

From a contemporary perspective, a deficiency of the book is that it is almost exclusively concerned with the toleration of those who share the Apostles' Creed, and the extent to which others should be tolerated is not always clear. (Compare, for example, William Penn's *The Great Case of Liberty of Conscience,* 1670.) However, certain passages suggest how the discussion could be expanded, particularly when he talks about the duty of a ruler to forbid "practices that cause harm, but not false opinions unless they lead to the dishonouring of God or civil disturbance" (8:144-45). In the twenty-first century this needs to be clarified, especially the issue of "dishonouring God," for there are many forms of anti-Christian or antireligious polemic that may be upsetting but that liberals, and indeed some more conservative Christians, would still not wish to be made illegal. Taylor marks a huge step in the direction of a tolerant society, but, not surprisingly, he was also a man of his time.

One of the other liberal emphases in Taylor is his approach to original sin. He is often referred to (e.g., by Samuel Taylor Coleridge[41]) as

---

41. In his *Aids to Reflection,* under the consideration of "Aphorism X," Coleridge has a considerable section devoted to Taylor's views. Overall, Coleridge is a great admirer of Taylor, but here he criticizes his views, referring to him as "the ablest and most formidable antagonist of this doctrine [i.e., of original sin]." Coleridge defends the doctrine, arguing that it is a kind of universal "fact" of human experience, but in my view Coleridge fails to make an adequate distinction between *peccatum* and *culpa.* I think that the Taylorian position can be much strengthened if one insists (as John Wesley did) that with the grace that is available, human beings can live without sin, and by adding that some people may have achieved a sinless state (even though this would not suffice to merit eternal life). Moreover, something akin to Taylor's position can be defended even if sin is universal, provided that one can reasonably claim that the sins of some people are relatively minor (in contrast with Calvin's claim that all sins, because directly or indirectly against God, deserve eternal punishment). It is true that many of the great-

someone who rejected that doctrine. In fact, however, if one looks at his writings carefully, it is the doctrine of original guilt that he attacks, while he clearly supports the kind of original sin teaching that I have defended here (and that is suggested in the Church of England Commission of 1922). In one of his letters he specifically says that he is not rejecting original sin, but that "which it is supposed to be" (9:368; cf. 9:1-25, 93-107). As in my account, Taylor emphasizes the weakness of human nature, especially when we consider its social aspect, which he likens to a fleet of ships colliding in a storm, and he shows how — in descendants of Adam and Eve — "sin was easy and ready at the door" (9:316-17).

Going back to the Greek text of Romans 5:12, Taylor strongly denies the attribution of guilt to infants.[42] He holds that the idea that we could be guilty because of what Adam did, and punished accordingly, is a challenge to the idea that God is just or good — in any meaningful sense. On this point, Taylor is unusually direct in his rejection of Calvinist teachings, with their implication that God is cruel (9:319). Chillingworth had not been quite that explicit, but in his account of infant baptism, he, too, strongly suggests that there is no guilt attributable to infants.[43] As we have seen, the Orthodox churches have always viewed the matter differently, but in the Latin church there were relatively few writers who had denied that infants could be born "guilty" (e.g., Julian, a fifth-century bishop of Eclanum, who was exiled for his alleged Pelagian beliefs, and, as

---

est saints have been profoundly aware of their sinfulness, but I venture to suggest that in some cases this is because they (rightly) take sin far more seriously than do ordinary people, not because their sins were actually greater. Once it is admitted that some people's sins are relatively small, the logic of the situation strongly suggests something like Taylor's position. For a discussion of Coleridge's argument, see Douglas Hedley, *Coleridge, Philosophy and Religion* (Cambridge, UK: Cambridge University Press, 2000), pp. 248-63.

42. In *Unum Necessarium* (1655) and *Deus Justificatus* (1656), Taylor, *Works,* 9:322, 351-52. A little later we find the same analysis of the Greek text in the Quaker apologist Robert Barclay, who says that our corrupted state is "not imputed to infants, until by transgression they actually joyn themselves therewith" (*An Apology for the True Christian Divinity* [London, 1678], the "fourth proposition" in the unpaginated preface; see also pp. 63-65 [p. 65 is erroneously paginated as 56]). The work first appeared in Latin (Amsterdam, 1676).

43. Chillingworth *The Religion of Protestants,* 7, 7, p. 390.

we have seen, Abelard). In the West, the extent to which Taylor (along with Chillingworth, the Quaker apologist Robert Barclay, and a few others, such as Henry Hallywell[44]) was ahead of his time in this matter can be seen from the fact that many Western theologians have distinguished between original sin and original guilt only in the last hundred years or so.

If Jeremy Taylor had had more knowledge of the Greek Orthodox tradition, he would have found strong ammunition for his rejection of original guilt within that tradition, which, as I have emphasized in chapter 2, never had to rely on the Vulgate's questionable translation of Saint Paul's Greek.

(10) Hannah Barnard

As in the cases of John Smith, the Cambridge Platonist, and William Chillingworth, of the Great Tew Circle, I have chosen Hannah Jenkins Barnard (1754-1825) as a representative of the Quakers, as well as for her individual contribution to that tradition, in this case as a representative of Quaker preachers, many of whom were women. (Among many other Quaker preachers, I was tempted to include John Woolman, the first significant figure in the antislavery movement, and Elizabeth Fry, with her seminal work in prisons.)

Barnard was born into a Baptist family in the state of New York but became a Quaker at about the time of her marriage (1779) and shortly afterwards was recognized by her meeting as a preacher. From 1798 to 1801, she went on a preaching tour of Great Britain, where she caused a scandal, particularly in the London meetinghouses, which at the time were dominated by an "evangelical" version of Quakerism. In 1802 this led to "disownment" by her local meeting back in Hudson, New York, as a result of the complaints that followed her from London.[45] However, she contin-

---

44. See Henry Hallywell, *Deus Justificatus* (London, 1668), originally published anonymously. This book contains a sustained attack on the "irrational doctrine" of "absolute reprobation." A less liberal aspect of Hallywell's writings concerns his generally unfair attack on contemporaneous Quakers.

45. This was the Quaker equivalent to "excommunication," which meant, in effect, that she lost her official recognition as a preacher.

ued her activities of writing and preaching (in a local "Peace Society," which she founded), and she still, on occasion, attended the Hudson Meeting.

Three of the lesser reasons for the complaints help to describe the character of Barnard, who was attractive and at the same time (according to all the evidence) both eloquent and "feisty." The first was her insistence, when visiting in a home of the Friends, that she would not sit down until the servants had been invited to join the family. The second was her support for the suggestion that meetinghouses should be made available to ministers of other denominations for their services, provided that Quakers could have equivalent opportunities to use their chapels. The third complaint concerned her voicing doubts about the importance of the virgin birth. However, the overriding reason for Barnard's scandal within Quakerism was her interpretation of pacifism, in which she maintained (along with a number of Irish Quakers whom she had met on her travels) that the killings carried out in the Jewish wars, especially those accompanying the occupation of the Holy Land, were not sanctioned by God.[46] In the book of Joshua, for example, when we read of God commanding the slaughter of enemies, including women, children, and animals, she said that this was not what God commanded but what they thought God commanded.

As I have already intimated, this issue is of enormous importance

---

46. Many Quakers, following the position of George Fox, maintain that all wars are wrong and that a follower of Jesus should never be actively involved in them. However, this has led to two misunderstandings of the Quaker tradition. First, most Quakers have not said that there could never be justified "violence" of any kind, for example, by a policeman making an arrest or parents defending their child. War is not like these examples because, in practice, it means killing the innocent as well as the attacker. Second, even in the seventeenth century, not all Quakers said that all war was wrong. Some of those who became Quakers had fought in Cromwell's army, though there was a tendency, after the end of the civil war, for a stronger line on pacifism to develop. Moreover, the influential Quaker Isaac Penington, a contemporary of Fox, defended purely defensive wars, notably when your country was invaded. It was aggressive and foreign war that he condemned. Obviously, the position of Penington, while attractive, raises difficulties that I cannot pursue here. For example, if a friendly and weak nation is attacked, for no good reason, why should we not come to its defense in the same way that we would defend ourselves? This would not mean an "aggressive" war, but it might well mean a "foreign" war.

because it is integrally connected with any coherent claim that God is good or just or loving. We have seen that Origen is sensitive to this issue, but he sidesteps it by insisting on the priority of the spiritual and moral meaning, while not actually asserting that the literal sense was false. In Castellio and John Smith, we have a clearer rejection of "verbal inspiration," but the problems posed by the book of Joshua are not dealt with so directly as they are by Hannah Barnard.

Since the time of Barnard, her response has become common among those who are eager to defend the justice of God; but as her history shows, it took a brave person to take this stand in her day.[47] It is interesting to note how similar brave voices are now emerging within liberal versions of Islam, which separate the core Qur'an (the "eternal message") from the "social" Qur'an, with the implication that much of the text should not be understood as verbally inspired.[48] Within some Muslim countries, this "heresy" could mean death.

Hannah Barnard's surviving writings also contain interesting comments on the Genesis 22 story in which Abraham is commanded to sacrifice his son, Isaac, only to have the boy's death averted at the last minute by the heavenly command to kill a ram that has its horns entangled in a nearby thicket. Her view parallels her view of the Joshua stories in that here, she claims, we see once again what the Jews *believed* God had commanded Abraham to do. Personally, I agree with Barnard's evaluation of the story in which the Israelites are commanded to kill all the men, women, and children of Ai; but I think that the Isaac story requires a more complex analysis.

In the first place, the picture of the ram being sacrificed instead of the son has huge symbolic significance, even if (as in my own case) one does not subscribe to the substitution theory of the atonement. At the very least, here is a powerful metaphor for the work of Christ. Furthermore, the story has more ambiguity within it than Barnard accounts for. For example, suppose that Abraham's faith is seen as a belief not simply

47. *Considerations on the Matter of the Difference between the Friends of London and Hannah Barnard* (Hudson, NY, 1802), Early American Imprints, 2nd series, 1839 (Worcester, MA: American Antiquarian Society, 1966), p. 13.

48. See Ghada Karmi, "Women, Islam and Patriarchalism," in M. Yamani, ed., *Feminism and Islam* (Reading, PA: Ithaca Press, 1996), pp. 80-81.

in the absolute right of God to command whatever he wants, but as belief that an ultimately righteous God will find a way either of avoiding the death of Isaac or of bringing him back to life. Perhaps this may be too subtle a way of interpreting what was in the mind of the historical Abraham, assuming that we think of the story as history. However, if — as I think is likely — we are dealing with a mixture of history and myth, similar considerations arise concerning how to interpret the story when we examine it as myth. As we saw in chapter 2, Kierkegaard regarded the story as a classic way of showing how the absolute demands of God could "suspend" the requirements of any "universal" morality. The "knight of faith" rises above the moral considerations that govern all those on a lower level. Critics of this interpretation, including myself, hold that this opens up a most dangerous way of justifying the grossest forms of cruelty in the name of religion, and they hold that history abounds with the dire consequences of this view of God's calling, a view that calls into question the very meaning of any claim that "God is good." On the other hand, supporters of Kierkegaard say that this liberal view renders God less than "the God of Abraham, Isaac, and Jacob," who has an absolute and unconditional right, as the Creator, to command what he chooses. The liberal view does not take seriously enough, so they might say, the actual experience of those who feel themselves to be in the divine presence.

Clearly, we have here a difficult question concerning how to balance (1) belief in a God who transcends the ordinary categories that describe our relationship with the world with (2) certain kinds of powerful personal experiences, and (3) with a rational reflection on how to interpret these experiences, either in our own lives or in those of others. With respect to apparent divine commands that appear to conflict with morality, I would pose the following question: How can we really *know* that this is a divine command, that is, once we accept the Christian belief that God is truly "the Good"? Overall, the discussion shows how complex the situation is and consequently how Barnard's view of the Abraham and Isaac story needs much amplification if it is to be upheld. (I will revisit this last subject in my discussion of Karl Barth in chapter 4 below.)

(11) J. F. D. Maurice

J. F. D. (John Frederick Denison) Maurice (1805-1872)[49] was one of many who were strongly influenced by Samuel Taylor Coleridge (who, if we were to concentrate on his later writings, could well have been another person on this list of exemplars).[50] At first glance, Maurice's life and writings might lead one to question whether he fits on this list of liberals, particularly because of his distaste of the word "liberal." There were two reasons for this distaste, both of which (paradoxically) strengthen the case for his inclusion, provided we bear in mind the eleven typical characteristics described in chapter 2.

The first was his intense disapproval of parties or sects within the church, and his principal critique of the "liberals" is in the context of his similar attack on the evangelical and Catholic *parties* within the church. He identifies the liberal "party" in the church as those who are antitheological and "ready to tolerate all opinions in theology."[51] As we have seen, this is not an accurate description of the tradition described in this book. But Maurice does say something that rings true for all of the thirteen exemplars I have chosen. The liberal tradition does not seek to be a separately organized sect or society in the church but a living tradition within every part of it. If, as a result of reading this book, Christians were to promote the liberal tradition by forming a new society within their own denomination, or within the ecumenical movement, this would be a response that I, for one, would regret. We have enough parties and sects and societies. It is much better for the ideas and examples from the liberal tradition to enter into the mindset of more and more people than to set up the tradition as some kind of rival group.

The second reason for Maurice's distaste for the term "liberal" was

---

49. His first initial, J. (for John), is often omitted from his initials. I suspect that this name was included in his initial baptism (Unitarian) but omitted from his second (and controversial) baptism (Anglican).

50. Among other influences, Coleridge's posthumous *Confessions of an Inquiring Spirit,* ed. H. St.-J. Hart (London: Black, 1840), helped to put forward liberal views concerning the inspiration of the Bible.

51. Quoted in Alex R. Vidler, *F. D. Maurice and Company* (London: SCM Press, 1966), p. 190.

its association, in his mind, with an extreme form of "individualism."[52] He was not opposed to human rights as the term that has become enshrined in recent declarations, but he insists that we must carefully distinguish being a person from being an individual, and that personal fulfillment needs to be in the context of a community of which Christ is the head. Infant baptism, he argues, is justifiable for this reason. Moreover, this emphasis on the headship of Christ is not restricted to active members of the Christian church. Within the new covenant, all people are related to the church, whether or not they recognize this truth, and all who respond to God are potentially beneficiaries of Christ's work. Christians are the ones who articulate and live this truth. He did not expound a complete universalism (as in at least one of Origen's writings), but he did harbor the hope that all might, in due time, be saved.

This sense of the "solidarity" of human beings is intimately connected with Maurice's involvement in the movement known as "Christian socialism," especially from 1848 to 1854. Socialism for Maurice was not necessarily connected with radical reform (though this might sometimes be necessary), nor with state ownership or control of economic affairs, and it is thus misleading to classify him as a socialist in the sense in which most people think of that term, despite his own use of the term. For him socialism meant "an order of society which encourages men to co-operate with one another instead of competing against one another; that is, it meant the opposite of individualism and *laissez-faire*."[53] Maurice's involvement with Christian socialism, along with his activities in the education of women and of working men, had a profound influence, but we do not have space to follow that involvement here.[54]

Maurice's approach to the Bible is also important with respect to the liberal tradition. Unlike some liberals of his time, he did accept the historicity of the story of Adam, and he rejected the revolutionary view of the Bible championed by Bishop Colenso — along with much of the move-

---

52. Vidler, *Maurice and Company,* pp. 73, 161-64.

53. Vidler, *Maurice and Company,* pp. 231-32.

54. In 1848, Maurice helped to found Queen's College for the education of women, and in 1854, the Working Men's College, of which he was the first principal. He strongly opposed university tests (which prevented non-Anglicans from attending some educational institutions).

ment known as "biblical criticism."[55] However, he was strongly opposed to what he called the "dogmatic" interpretation of Scripture, in which the Bible is quarried in order to support a particular system or used as a series of proof-texts rather than being seen as a whole story.[56] Also, as we have already noted, he rejected any literal interpretation of hellfire because it was to him simply incompatible with the love of God.

Overall, Maurice is one of those influential figures that do not fit comfortably into any category, including, as I have intimated, that of liberal. Nevertheless, he has had a profound influence on the tradition I am concerned with, including the way in which theological theory is held to be linked with practical life — in his case, with support for a version of Christian socialism. Here I shall mention just one other liberal aspect of his influence: the way in which he sought to see some truth within the views that he rejected. For example, he dismisses the Calvinist account of election, but he holds that it is a distortion of a truth rather than mere error. As Alec Vidler puts it (referring to Maurice's position), "Calvinism witnesses, though in a perverse way, to the fundamental truth that salvation is grounded in God's choice of man and not in man's choice of God."[57]

(12) Joseph Lightfoot

With Lightfoot, I have again chosen a figure who is representative of a group, in this case the famous Cambridge trio of philosopher-theologians who dominated Cambridge theology in the mid- to late nineteenth century, the other two being B. F. Westcott and F. J. A. Hort. I must also emphasize that none of the three was an out-and-out liberal, as we can see, for example, from their dislike of many of the ideas expressed in *Essays*

---

55. John William Colenso (1814-1883) was a gifted mathematician before becoming the bishop of Natal. His writings on the Pentateuch — in which he rejected the belief that it was written by Moses — caused a storm. Among other important and influential views were his rejection of eternal punishment and his support for oppressed aboriginal peoples.

56. Vidler, *F. D. Maurice and Company*, pp. 141, 147-51.

57. Vidler, *F. D. Maurice and Company*, p. 59.

and Reviews (1860), a book that scandalized a large number of more conservative Christians at the time of its publication. However, in both their study of the early fathers and their biblical scholarship, they introduced a new era of exegesis, rooted in a wide-ranging scholarship that included an intimate knowledge of Latin, Greek, and Hebrew. Their scholarship had a strong influence on the development of liberal theology.

In the case of Joseph B. Lightfoot (1828-1889), who was the bishop of Durham at the end of his life, I shall emphasize two aspects of his influence.

First, there is his role in the gradual recognition of the role of women in the ministry of the church. The New Testament mentions "deaconesses," but conservative Catholics and Protestants have often insisted that these were not female "deacons," referring to one of the three major orders of ministry that developed within the church (bishop, priest, and deacon), but rather an altogether lower order. Lightfoot, on scholarly grounds, questions this, and includes many women among the active members of the diaconate in the early church.[58] (More recently, the Catholic scholar John Wijngaards has provided additional evidence for this conclusion.[59])

Second, in a long essay added to his *Commentary on Philippians,* he discusses the relationship of the different officers in the early church, and this discussion has become seminal reading for any subsequent work. Several important matters arise in the essay that have implications for the liberal tradition. Lightfoot claims that there is no evidence that in the first years of the church there was any hierarchical difference between bishops (*episkopoi* in Greek, which literally means "overseers") and priests (*presbuteroi,* or "elders"). The bishop was simply one of the priests, or presbyters, perhaps the one who looked after correspondence with other churches (though this is a later suggestion). The bishops did not make up an "order" above presbyters; instead, some presbyters moved to a more supervisory role, though not via any form of ordination.

58. J. B. Lightfoot, *The Christian Ministry* (a dissertation appended to his *Saint Paul's Epistle to the Philippians,* rev. ed. [London: Macmillan, 1896]), p. 191.

59. John Wijngaards, *No Women in Holy Orders? The Women Deacons of the Early Church* (Norwich, UK: Canterbury Press, 2002). "The undeniable historical reality is that women *were* admitted to the full and sacramental diaconate" (p. 147, italics in original).

Lightfoot himself thought that this movement began during the lives of the apostles, but many scholars suspect that it did not become common practice until the middle of the second century. In any case, the famous "three-fold ministry" of bishop, priest, and deacon represents general church practice in the second — but not the first — century. This account has major implications for conservative Catholic views concerning the "apostolic succession." It does not render it meaningless, but it certainly does question the version of it that emphasizes an unbroken line of *bishops* from apostolic times.[60]

This context illuminates the continuing debate concerning whether Christian ministers should be referred to as "priests," "presbyters," "elders," "pastors," or in some other way, given the fact that, according to the New Testament, the Jewish priesthood (the *hieroi,* those who offered sacrifices in the Temple) was not continued within Christianity, except — symbolically — in terms of the office of Christ and the role of the church collectively. Strictly speaking, the term "presbyter" is closest to the Greek term used in the New Testament *(presbuteros),* which, as we have seen, is most accurately translated as "elder." However, this term is not without its problems because of the baggage it carries in many people's minds,

---

60. The conservative view is that there needs to be (1) an unbroken line of "laying on of hands" from one bishop to another from the very first bishops, and (2) that the first bishops received the laying on of hands from the apostles. If Lightfoot is right, the early church might well have recognized an apostolic succession of presbyters, but not of bishops. If this is the implication of New Testament scholarship, John Wesley would have been justified in his famous appointment of bishops to work in America — those who were ordained by presbyters but not bishops. A compromise position (and my own) is that we should admit that the apostolic succession of bishops is probably a second-century innovation, but that, nevertheless, we should seek to maintain it, if possible, as a valuable and traditional symbol of our links to the early church. This view renders the debate between Canterbury and Rome on the validity of Anglican orders less significant, though even on the assumptions of conservative views, there is much to be said for the validity of Anglican orders. A key objection, according to the Vatican's statement of 1896, is the inadequacy of the form of service used to ordain Archbishop Parker in 1559 with respect to intention. However, the Anglican response pointed to the clear indication, in the preface to the 1552 ordinal used, that the *intention* was to make a bishop, in the traditional sense. This central point is often neglected in subsequent discussions. See the *Answer of the Archbishops of England to the Apostolic Letter of Pope Leo XIII* (1897), in *Anglican Orders* (London: SPCK, 1932), pp. 48-49.

given its close association with the Calvinist or near-Calvinist system associated with "Presbyterianism." The difficulty in finding the best term is more than academic, because Muslims and many others object that Christians need the intermediary of a "priest," while they can have direct access to God.

Lightfoot prefers the term "presbyter" to that of priest, but points out that colloquially (in English) the word "priest" can refer to two very different functions, "the minister who presides over and instructs a Christian congregation," and "the offerer of sacrifices" (equivalent to the Greek *hiereus*).[61] Many liberals dislike the term "priest" because it suggests something too close to the ancient Jewish priesthood, and thus it does seem to deny the adequacy of every individual's direct relationship with God. My own view is that, strictly speaking, the term is inappropriate, but that because of traditional usage we probably have to live with it, and that this is acceptable if we emphasize Lightfoot's first sense of the term.

Finally, there is the relationship of the New Testament apostles to the overseers and presbyters. Lightfoot's view is that in the apostolic age the apostles "held no local office," with the possible exception of James (Jesus' brother).[62] He might properly be regarded as both an apostle and as bishop of Jerusalem — in the very different situation of the Jewish Christian church.[63] In this context Lightfoot does not discuss Saint Peter's relationship with the church in Rome, but other scholars argue that, while Peter probably died in Rome (ca. 65 CE), there is no evidence that he held the office of bishop there. That he did so became a pious belief that helped to enhance the authority of the Roman church, but the first clear statement of the claim comes in a letter by Irenaeus from about 200 CE.[64] Many liberals have no problem

---

61. Lightfoot, *The Christian Ministry*, p. 189.

62. In the New Testament the term "apostle" is not only used for the twelve disciples appointed by Jesus, but also for other key missionaries, such as Paul and Barnabas.

63. Lightfoot, *The Christian Ministry*, pp. 196-97.

64. On this matter, the first epistle of Clement, who may have been pope in about 90-100 CE, is often cited. However, although there is, in my view, a probability that this letter is genuine, and that it indicates how the Roman church was seeking to exert some leadership with regard to the church in Corinth, there is no appeal to authority based on Peter's alleged status in Rome.

with the idea of giving the bishop of Rome a special status, both because of the historical importance of Rome as a Christian center and because of a genuine connection between the city and Saint Peter. However, claims to be *the* "vicar of Christ," directly descended from Peter as the first bishop of Rome, let alone claims to hold a certain kind of infallibility, are quite different.[65]

(13) Frederick Temple

Frederick Temple (1821-1902) went to Balliol College, Oxford, where he achieved a double first in mathematics and classics. Later, as a fellow of the same college, he was one of the few contemporary theologians who studied German philosophy, including the works of Kant. After working on educational reform, which was a lifelong interest, he became headmaster of Rugby in 1857, where, among other changes, he introduced both science and music into the curriculum. While there, he contributed to the infamous *Essays and Reviews,* which, as I have noted earlier, produced a sensation on its publication in 1860. (J. F. D. Maurice, in some ways a conservative on matters of biblical inspiration, was among its critics.) Despite hostility toward him from both the evangelical and high-church wings of the Church of England, Temple became the bishop of Exeter and finally Archbishop of Canterbury.

One of his contributions to the liberal tradition was, of course, his support for natural science and particularly his acceptance of a Darwinian account of evolution. As early as 1860, he preached a sermon at Oxford University in which he laid out the essentials of a positive understanding between science and religion. Although he does not deal directly with biological evolution in that sermon (Darwin's *The Origin of Species* was published the year before), he says: "[T]here seems no more reason why the solar system should not have been brought into its present form by the slow working of natural causes than the surface of the

65. The doctrine of papal infallibility (1870) restricts the infallible statements to those made ex cathedra, that is, to proclamations made after a formal process of consultation. According to many commentators, infallible statements include the bulls that declare the decisions of ecumenical councils.

earth, about whose gradual formation most students are now agreed."[66] Here, in the acceptance of "the slow working of nature," as opposed to miraculous intervention, we have exactly the approach that liberal theologians would soon apply to biological evolution. The reference to "the surface of the earth" harks back to the disputes over geology, begun early in the century, in which liberal Christians increasingly had come to accept that the biblical "days" of creation referred to eons (or, e.g., in Gladstone, "chapters") rather than periods of twenty-four hours.[67] More importantly, the Bible was a book of religious and moral meaning rather than of natural science. A little later in the sermon he discusses how, whenever there is a clash between "a treatise on physics" and a "treatise on theology and morals," it is simply a question of evidence. Hence: "In the case of Galileo the question has been answered; the astronomer was right, the theologians wrong."[68]

Temple returned to these themes in his much larger Bampton Lectures of 1884, where he makes direct references to Darwin. Noting how evolutionary theory had compelled theologians to change their views, he writes: "The difference is that the execution of that [divine] purpose belongs more to the original act of creation, less to acts of governance since."[69]

This quotation raises a general point about liberal views of providence. As we have seen in chapter 2, the belief that God directly arranges every physical event, like the controller pulling the strings of a marionette, has long been rejected in favor of a view in which, as Austin Farrer has put it, "God makes the world make itself." However, the opposite of the marionette view, in which — as in purely materialistic accounts — God has no impact on cosmic or human events, is also rejected by the

66. Frederick Temple, *The Present Relations of Science to Religion* (Oxford, 1860), p. 7.

67. W. E. Gladstone, *The Impregnable Rock of Holy Scripture* (London: Isbister, 1892), p. 56. In this book Gladstone accepts evolutionary ideas of the formation of the earth, but he retains fairly conservative views concerning the Old Testament account of human history.

68. Temple, *The Present Relations*, p. 14.

69. Frederick Temple, *The Relations between Religion and Science* (London: Macmillan, 1884), pp. 122-23.

Christian tradition. What, then, is the mechanism by which providence operates? Obviously, if God is to be God, we cannot expect to give a comprehensive answer to this question, but we should at least be able to give some intimations on which faith and reason can work. Here we have a choice: either (as in the quotation from Temple) to put our emphasis on the way in which, perhaps at the "big bang," God has endowed the natural order with such a dynamic nature that the gradual emergence of intelligent life is inevitable; or to claim that God is active *within* the workings of nature (and human minds), but by a kind of influence that is more akin to persuasion — as in Whitehead's thought — than to force or miracle. A third view would be to claim, as Isaac Newton did, that every now and then God adjusts the workings of nature. However, this view seems far less satisfactory. Personally, I am a little uneasy with the Temple quote because liberal Christians should try to emphasize the involvement of providence in *both* the original act of creation and the ongoing life of the universe. God is acting creatively in the present as well as in the past.

Here I shall make just one suggestion within a debate that would take us far beyond the confines of this book. We are increasingly aware that any adequate account of human action, including what we mean by "freedom" and "autonomy," has to see the human body as a complex whole. It is neither a case of a purely spiritual mind governing a purely physical body, nor vice versa, but a complex set of interrelationships. Both Cartesian and purely materialistic accounts of human action are suspect. Similarly, any adequate explanation of the evolution of the cosmos may require an understanding of complex interrelationships, and if there is a loving, creative source of the whole universe, it would be absurd to rule out the providential power of this source, both in its initiation and in its daily activity. As I have suggested earlier, the Acts of the Apostles reads like a "saga of the Holy Spirit," because even without the introduction of the miraculous, if there is a divine source of the world, and if we walk "in tune" with this loving source, the world may seem — and actually become — a very different place.

To return to Frederick Temple: as with many exemplars of a tradition, he is not an unqualified supporter, in his case because of his active and lifelong support of the temperance movement and because of his intolerance concerning the use of incense and the reservation of the sacrament for those churches that wanted to maintain these Catholic practices. However, in addition to his view of science, there are several other liberal credentials, including his support for the University Tests Bill (1870) and the opening of churchyards (1876), thus removing unfair restrictions on those who were not members of the Church of England. He also supported the growth of lay participation in the activities of the church, especially in terms of representation. On social issues, we find a shift from an early Toryism to a general support for many of the liberal policies associated with Gladstone.

B. Twentieth-century Themes

I have ended the last section with Frederick Temple because the primary focus of this book is the history of the liberal tradition up to about 1900, even though there were many significant liberal theologians in the twentieth century. Subsequent liberals have made useful contributions to the themes (or "typical characteristics") outlined in chapter 2, as well as to at least five additional ones that gained prominence in the twentieth century, though none of these issues was entirely new. These issues warrant a more extended treatment, but here I shall only briefly indicate their nature.

Any adequate list of twentieth-century theologians who have made significant contributions to liberal theology would be very long, and would also run the risk of making a generally artificial distinction between a set of heroes and nonheroes. Such a distinction might make sense with respect to the past, when extremely divisive issues, such as the toleration of alternative beliefs, were so sharp; but it would be unhelpful now, when there is such a wide range of theologies on offer, nearly all of which would support toleration. Furthermore, while some theologians would clearly fall within the criteria (such as Keith Ward and Richard Harries), there are a number of significant theologians who would support many but not all of the eleven typical characteristics of the tradition outlined in chapter 2. (Alvin Plantinga would probably fall into this category.)

Rather than producing a list of "approved" liberal theologians, it would probably be more helpful to have a list of those different voices, each of whom have something important to say to the tradition, whether or not they should be classed as supporters of mainstream Christianity (in either its conservative or liberal forms). For example, although Gordon Kaufman is frequently referred to as a "liberal" theologian, he is a good example of a significant theologian who would not be a typical exemplar of the kind of liberal orthodoxy I have here described, among other reasons because of his approach to revelation, especially in his later writings. (Gary Dorrien, summarizing one aspect of Kaufman's thought, writes: "It was simply wrong to claim that theology rests on God's revelation."[70]) However, it is still true, I suggest, that Kaufman provides a voice with which liberal theology must engage.[71] We might underscore the contributions of Herbert Hensley Henson and William Temple in the early part of the twentieth century; more recent examples — all of whom have made specific contributions to the topics highlighted in this book — should include Basil Mitchell,[72] Douglas Hedley,[73] and Sarah Coakley.[74]

70. Gary Dorrien, *The Making of American Liberal Theology* (Louisville: Westminster John Knox, 2006), 3:313.

71. For example, Kaufman's forceful presentation of the case for theology as an imaginative "construction" has to be balanced, in my view, with a continuing respect for revelation. See esp. Gordon D. Kaufman, *An Essay on Theological Method,* rev. ed. (Ann Arbor, MI: Scholars Press, 1979), p. 43. In his earlier *Systematic Theology* (New York: Scribner, 1968), Kaufman defends a more traditional account of revelation, though one rooted in personal encounter rather than propositions.

72. See, e.g., Basil Mitchell, "Revelation Revisited," in Sarah Coakley and David A. Palin, eds., *The Making and Remaking of Christian Doctrine* (Oxford: Clarendon Press, 1993), which supports a liberal acceptance of the idea of revelation (that I have defended in chaps. 1 and 2). This theme helps to highlight the inadequacy of the article on liberalism in the 2nd edition of the *New Catholic Encyclopedia* (New York: Gale, 2003), which sees the principal feature of liberal theology as "emancipation from supernatural demands."

73. See, e.g., Douglas Hedley, *Coleridge, Philosophy and Religion* (Cambridge, UK: Cambridge University Press, 2000). Hedley's work on the imagination is relevant to any adequate account of what we mean by rationality, and particularly its relationship to intuition and will. Hedley's reflections on Coleridge are also important in the context of positive Christian responses to the Enlightenment.

74. See, e.g., Sarah Coakley, "Why Three? Some Further Reflections on the Origins

THE TRADITION OF LIBERAL THEOLOGY

The first theme that gained a new prominence in the twentieth century was that of theological reflection on new data concerning human
sexuality and gender. The eleventh theme explored in chapter 2 ("a range
of acceptable lifestyles") indicated how liberal theologians have begun to
respond to the issues raised. (I will revisit the issues in my discussion of
Karl Barth in chapter 4.) Another example is the need to question the
conservative claim that everyone is made "either male or female" by the
Creator (reflecting a literal reading of Genesis 1:27), when recent studies
expose the genuine incidence of intersexuality, in some cases (as in "true
chimaerism") with both x and y chromosomes distributed throughout
the human body.

Second, there is the related theme of the role of women in the ministry of the church (as foreshadowed in the Quaker doctrine — from about
1650 — of the total equality of men and women, and in some of the teachings of Joseph Lightfoot). The disciples of Jesus were clearly both men
and women. In contrast, the twelve apostles were all men, but given the
fact that this was a group of disciples who traveled around with Jesus,
sometimes probably "sleeping rough," it is difficult to draw any theological conclusions concerning the maleness of ministry from this. In the
postapostolic age, three orders of ministry developed, but we have seen
that there are strong grounds for holding that one of them, the *episkopoi,*
was not a higher order than that of *presbuteroi* until the second century.
Meanwhile, it is likely that the *diakonoi* (deacons) was made up of both
men and women (probably including Phoebe, who is mentioned in Rom.
16:1). On the other hand, it may well be that in the early church both the
expanded order of apostles (which included Paul and Barnabas) and the
order of *presbuteroi* were either wholly or primarily men. There is some
scholarly dispute on this matter, for example, concerning the status of
Junia (Rom. 16:7); the Greek makes it unclear whether she was known
among the apostles in the sense of being known *to* them or *as one of*
them. Likewise, some early Christian paintings may show women as

---

of the Doctrine of the Trinity," in Coakley and Palin, *The Making and Remaking of Christian Doctrine.* Here (within a friendly critique of Maurice Wiles) Coakley defends a traditional Trinitarianism in the context of the Christian experience of prayer. This she links,
in an interesting way, with suggestions about the development of the triadic baptismal
formula (of Matt. 28:19) in the light of the special gifts of the Holy Spirit (pp. 41-42).

presbuteroi or *episkopoi*. If I am correct in thinking that in the early church women were rarely, if ever, either apostles or elders, those who support the ordination of women to the priesthood are likely to use two kinds of argument. The first is that first-century practice is not always a guide to what is appropriate for the twenty-first; the second — and more radical — approach is to suggest that the early church got this wrong and failed to see the full implications of the teachings of Jesus. Even Saint Paul may not have realized the full import of his own pronouncement that in Christ "there is neither Jew nor Greek, neither bond nor free, neither male nor female" (Gal. 3:28), which, as many have pointed out, may be a direct response to the ancient Jewish prayer of men when they thank God for being Jewish, free, and male. Conservative Christians, and likewise many Muslims, tend to claim that men and women are "equal but different." This is an initially plausible starting point, but when the list of differences is alleged to point to leadership qualities being primarily male, then liberals get very suspicious. Our experience of women's leadership in both politics and religion may indicate some differences of approach, but certainly not of quality.

A third area of unfinished business for the liberal tradition, in which every generation has to reinterpret the gospel for the times in which it is preached, includes further reflection on the scientific milieu. In the nineteenth century, when several of the exemplars reviewed in this chapter lived, there were, I would argue, at least two major scientific breakthroughs that had obvious implications for theology. Early in that century there were huge advances in geology, implying a new understanding of the age of the world, and these prompted the remarks Frederick Temple made in his sermon of 1860 at Oxford; just a year earlier, 1859 saw the publication of Darwin's *On the Origin of Species*. Neither of these advances, in my view, pose fundamental challenges to the heart of the Christian gospel when this is properly understood, but they certainly challenge naïve and fundamentalist versions of it, and they have certainly led to more nuanced ways of describing both creation and the traditional "argument from design." In the nineteenth century there were other major advances, including Faraday's work in electromagnetism, but these did not have such an obvious impact on theology.

In the twentieth century perhaps the greatest scientific advances surround Einstein's papers of 1905 and 1915 (concerning special and general relativity); the advent of quantum mechanics, notably from 1926; the "big bang" theory of the origins of the universe in the 1960s; and the discovery of DNA in the 1980s. (Perhaps we should include Freud's work, early in the century, on the role of the unconscious mind; but within the field of psychology there is much more disagreement than is true of discoveries within the field of physics.) Once again, in my view, none of these advances challenges the fundamentals of Christian belief, but they all call for a considered response, especially among scientists with Christian convictions who fully understand these aspects of contemporary science. In each case, it may turn out that certain traditional doctrines have to be expressed in new and different ways, as in the case of the argument from design.[75] This leads to work in progress that will be of special interest to the liberal tradition and that may illuminate the gospel in all kinds of unforeseeable ways. However, that is not the burden of this book.

In general, the liberal tradition in Christian theology has had little conflict with science, as the early acceptance of Darwinian ideas by the likes of Frederick Temple indicates. An interesting illustration of this is the way in which post-Reformation Anglicans tended to support "scientific" medicine, for example, in the life of Stephen Hales (1677-1761), who integrated his work as a country clergyman with his scientific work, notably in the area of medicine.[76] In addition to his pioneering work on blood pressure and nerves and ventilation, he was actively involved in both preventive and community medicine, which were of direct relevance to the well-being of his parishioners. A considerable number of clergy actually combined the roles of priest and physician, and this kind

75. In my book *Unblind Faith* (2nd ed., 2010), chap. 14, I have given an example of how this traditional argument can still be used within the context of a full acceptance of Darwinism. The argument, as reformulated, no longer tries to argue that complex structures, such as the eye, cannot be explained without an active designer, but (among other things) points rather to the extraordinary capacity of nature to produce reflective beings, such as ourselves, and to the appropriate sense of wonder at the very existence of such an order.

76. See I. B. Smith, "The Impact of Stephen Hales on Medicine," *Journal of the Royal Society of Medicine* 86 (1993): 349-52.

of union contrasted with how the nonestablished denominations were more likely to approve forms of faith healing.[77] The evidence suggests that this interconnection was due, in part, to the general Anglican reliance on "the argument from design," which encouraged the expectation that providence would normally work through the "natural order" of things.

The idea that science and religion form two different and essentially noncompeting areas of human endeavor has its attractions, and has enabled many persons of science to combine their professional work with a serious commitment to a religious way of life — in Christian or other forms. More generally, we have to be wary of attempts to apply scientific methodology, because of its spectacular successes, to all other intellectual disciplines. It would be absurd to treat the academic study of history in exactly the same way as the study of physics, notwithstanding some cases of overlap (e.g., with the use of radiocarbon dating). Both disciplines develop their own methods of critical inquiry. More controversially, I would say the same thing about, say, anthropology and musicology, and — to approach the case at hand — philosophy and theology. All of these disciplines can be both critical and rational, but in different ways, and each has to respond to the special features of its particular subject matter. Nevertheless, I suspect that on occasions there is a case for some active engagement across the disciplines, and that too limited a relationship, in which scientists and theologians always keep carefully to their own fields of inquiry, may be inadvisable. In principle, there could be occasions when work in one field really does challenge or illuminate work in another, and in the past, when this appears to have been the case, creative sparks have sometimes flown.

Accordingly, contemporary work in the neurosciences may challenge or illuminate accounts of what it is to be human, and some writers who either are or have been scientists (according to one's point of view) seriously challenge what are alleged to be the materialistic assumptions of much contemporary science. An example of the latter is the work of Rupert Sheldrake, and it is interesting to note the generally hostile reac-

77. See Michael Langford, "Moral Demands and Medical Practice," in D. W. Hardy and P. H. Sedgwick, eds., *The Weight of Glory* (Edinburgh: T&T Clark, 1991).

tion to his work among scientists, especially to his recent book *The Science Delusion.*[78] I do not think that all those who can properly be called liberal theologians can be expected to have a common mind on such conflicts, because this may be one of many legitimate areas of disagreement or uncertainty. But if it is true, as is alleged, that some leading scientists refuse even to examine the evidence that Sheldrake brings forward, then there must be a worry that certain a priori assumptions, which are actually in conflict with the scientific tradition, are clouding genuine objectivity.

The fourth theme concerns further reflection on the relationship of the gospel to modern forms of capitalism. Such reflection has an ancient pedigree: for example, Augustine's discussion of the relationship of the church to the Roman Empire; the medieval discussions of the proper role of money; J. F. D. Maurice's concern with a Christian form of socialism; and Christian reflections on the issue of a "just wage."[79] Anything that intimately affects the lives of ordinary people needs to be reflected on in the context of the Christian gospel.[80]

A fifth area of reflection concerns the relationship of Christianity to nonhuman animals and, more generally, to the environment. Once again, this deserves a separate and extended treatment, one that could begin with the significant contribution of Gordon Kaufman to this area of theology.[81]

78. Rupert Sheldrake, *The Science Delusion* (London: Coronet, 2012). See, e.g., the generally negative review by John Greenbank in *Philosophy Now* 93 (November/December 2012), and the generally positive review by Mary Midgley in *The Guardian* (January 27, 2012).

79. For an interesting study of this subject, see James Healey, S.J., *The Just Wage: 1750-1890* (The Hague: Nijhoff, 1966).

80. See, e.g., Eve Poole, *The Church on Capitalism* (Basingstoke, UK: Palgrave Macmillan, 2010).

81. See Gordon D. Kaufman, *Theology for a Nuclear Age* (Manchester, UK: Manchester University Press, 1985).

CHAPTER FOUR

Some Alternatives to Liberal Christian Theology

───o‰o───

A. Introduction

For the most part, the first three chapters have been positive in the sense of saying what liberal theology stands for rather than what it denies. Where comments have been negative, it has usually been when I have drawn a contrast to conservative forms of Christian belief in either the Catholic or the Protestant traditions. The purpose of the negative writing has not been destructive, but the need to highlight liberal views by contrasting them with others. In the first part of this chapter, I shall expand further on liberalism's contrast to conservative forms of Christianity, and then I shall continue the exploration of liberal theology in the context of contemporary materialism. In the last section of this chapter, I shall consider some of the issues that divide liberal Christians from followers of other great religions. However, I shall not include a general review of the great non-Christian religions in that section, partly because I have already intimated a response to several of those religions in my book *Unblind Faith,*and partly because any adequate treatment of this subject would require a much larger work.[1] Instead of reviewing particu-

1. Michael J. Langford, *Unblind Faith,* 2nd ed. (Aldershot: Parapress, 2010; [1st ed. London: SCM Press, 1982]).

lar religions, I shall instead consider some of the more general issues that arise within interfaith dialogue.

I close these introductory comments with an indication of why I hesitated to include this chapter; it is precisely because of the relatively negative tone that inevitably accompanies any criticism of alternative points of view. If I were asked to give a public lecture on why I disagree with X, where X represents a system of beliefs that is held by many intelligent and sincere people (e.g., traditional Roman Catholic teaching), I would try to begin with what we share in common before moving on to any critique. This sharing might be represented by the following series of affirmations that could be made by typical followers of what I have described as the liberal tradition:

1. With all human beings of good will we share a sense that there is a spiritual dimension to life that is more important than the purely material. When properly understood, this is common ground with many of those who call themselves atheists or secular humanists.

2. With all followers of the great religions we share not only the first affirmation, but also the belief that there can be positive benefits from commitment to a way of life in which one can find a place for communal forms of ritual expression, and (in most cases) a special reverence for certain places and writings and spiritual leaders from which we can learn.

3. With all other monotheists we share a belief that there is a creative power at work within the universe that has some analogy to the concepts of "mind" and "intelligence" and "love," as experienced in human life at its most fulfilled.

4. With all other followers of the Abrahamic religions we share a belief that God has been active (among other ways) within the experience of the Judaic tradition, especially in matters such as the nature of God ("I am who I am") and the call to act with justice and love in response to the word of God.

5. With all other followers of the Christian tradition we share a commitment to Jesus as Lord, as in the first article of the creed, "Jesus is Lord," or the variant "Jesus is the Christ" (made explicit in Acts 2:38; 8:16; 10:48; 19:4-5; 22:16; cf. 2:36 and 18:28). Furthermore, if we are

within what I have called "mainstream Christianity," we believe that God is known to us in three particular ways; first, as Creator (or Father); second, as represented in a particular human image (or Son); and third, as an extraordinary source of spiritual energy, both in others and within ourselves (or Spirit).

6. We share with other followers of the (deliberately lowercase) "catholic" tradition within Christianity a commitment to a form of Christianity that seeks: (a) understanding as well as faith *(fides quaerens intellectum)*, because the Fall, while accepted as a powerful — indeed, a "true" — metaphor, is not seen as involving the total depravity of the human mind; (b) a positive approach to the good and beautiful things in the world, which opens up a sacramental approach to life; (c) a positive approach to the institution of the church, as both human and (in calling) divine, an approach that combines a realistic critique of its many failings with a commitment to its work and, in many cases, a love for what it can bring to us.

Only in the context of these positive affirmations would I want to proceed with the criticisms of certain Christian (or other) beliefs, all of which should be understood in this more general context.

B. Conservative Forms of Christianity

(1) Fundamentalism

The most obvious form of Christian conservatism rejected by the liberal tradition is generally called "fundamentalism." Unfortunately, this is an ambiguous term, and when it is taken to mean support for a few "fundamental" doctrines, then no objection need be made. In practice, however, the term is usually applied to a pivotal belief in the *verbal* inspiration of the Bible, and this, for a whole series of reasons that I have already sketched, is rejected by liberal theology — especially in the last two hundred years. One reason for this rejection is the problems it introduces with respect to the goodness and justice of God. Another reason is a questioning of whether God speaks to people today, in our own experience, in this direct way — at least in typical cases. As we have seen, this point about verbal inspiration should not be identified with claims about the historical accuracy of the whole Bible (though they are often connected), because it is quite possible to believe that the story of Adam, for example, is verbally inspired but not literal history, on the grounds that it is a verbally inspired parable. Typically, liberals reject both the doctrine of verbal inspiration and the total historicity of the whole Bible, but these two issues should not be confused. (I have already discussed the subject of the verbal inspiration of the Bible, both in the second chapter and in the third chapter in the subsections on Origen, John Smith, and Hannah Barnard.)

In addition to issues concerning the verbal inspiration and the historicity of the Bible, fundamentalism is often associated with a doctrine of the atonement, or redemption, that is characterized by variations on Anselm's "substitution" theory. (I have discussed this issue in several places, notably in chapter 2 under the subheading "A Nonlegalist Account of Redemption" and in the subsection on Abelard in chapter 3.) Frequently, this approach to atonement theory goes with a "black and white" view of humanity, though the interconnection may be as much a matter of psychology as of theology. Here there is a radical separation between the true believers, who are saved, and the rest of humanity, who are damned. This "black and white" approach can easily be supported by some biblical passages, for example, the parables of the wheat and the chaff and of the sheep and the goats. However, I would claim that those who preach this radical division tend to forget the wider biblical context in which such stark categories are balanced by many other factors. For example, even in the Old Testament the story of Naaman the leper (2 Kings 5) shows sensitivity to those who, outwardly, take part in idolatrous worship, provided their hearts are in the right place. In the New Testament there are numerous references to those outside the strict community of followers who are not condemned (e.g., "He that is not against us is for us," Luke 9:50). Paradoxically, perhaps the most striking example is Jesus' parable of the sheep and the goats (Matt. 25), where the sheep are not necessarily those who *call* Jesus Lord, but are those who feed the hungry, clothe the naked, visit those in prison, and so on. My own view is that the "black and white" parables, in their full context, are not references to an absolute divide between people but rather are references to the urgency of our response to "the good, the true, and the beautiful," and to the unique opportunities to respond to an urgent need at a particular moment and place. The directness of the challenge is there, but the human response is multifaceted. Further, in many cases the black and white passages should be seen in terms of a kind of hyperbole that characterized much moral teaching in the ancient world. We all recognize that when Jesus spoke of the beam in our own eye and the mote in others' eyes, or — even more evidently — when he spoke of a potential need to "hate" our families for his sake (Luke 14:26), he was using this traditional teaching method. Yet some fundamentalist Christians continue to treat individual verses in the Bible as if they could be interpreted literally — and without considering the broader context.

I shall end this section with a comment on the "evangelical" wing of the Christian churches (as found within many denominations). Sometimes there is an overlap with fundamentalism, but in many cases those who call themselves "evangelicals" would dissociate themselves from some or all of the doctrines I have linked with the former term. As I have already indicated, "evangelical" simply means "a bearer of the good news" in its literal meaning, and as such, all Christians should see themselves as evangelicals. However — again, in practice — the term often goes with a set of beliefs, some of which liberal Christians will fully endorse and some of which will strike alarm. For example, the "Evangelical Alliance's Basis of Faith 1970" statement includes these items: "5. The universal sinfulness and guilt of fallen man, making him subject to God's wrath and condemnation. 6. The substitutionary sacrifice of the incarnate Son of God as the sole all-sufficient ground of redemption from the guilt and power of sin." As we have seen, mainstream Christians who support the whole of the Apostles' Creed can legitimately challenge these two statements on both biblical and rational grounds, at least if they are interpreted — as they usually are — to imply any original guilt attributable to the newborn. That said, the opposition to such beliefs (which are held by some of, but by no means all of, those who call themselves evangelicals) must be put in the context of a shared belief in the Lordship of Christ and in a loving God who has revealed himself as Father, Son, and Spirit, and in admiration for the genuine enthusiasm and warmth of many evangelical communities who witness, sometimes in dangerous places, to the overriding importance of love.

(2) Magisterium

A second form of conservatism that is generally rejected by liberal theology is what is considered to be an inappropriate emphasis on authority, especially when this authority is claimed to be in some way derived from God. Sometimes this objection is made to the power or prestige that is accorded to certain Protestant writers or preachers; but more often the objection is directed at the way in which the Roman Catholic *magisterium* (i.e., its teaching authority) is interpreted.

The term "magisterium" is used in different ways, and since the time of the first Vatican Council (1870), it has commonly been divided into the more formal "solemn judgment" of the church (sometimes referred to as the "extraordinary magisterium") and the somewhat lower category of the "ordinary magisterium." According to most interpretations, the former includes not only the three "infallible" statements, made ex cathedra after a special process of consultation (*Ineffabilis Deus,* the 1854 bull defining the Immaculate Conception of Mary; *Pastor Aeternus,* the 1870 bull defining the doctrine of infallibility itself; and *Munificentissimus Deus,* the 1950 bull declaring the bodily Assumption of Mary), but also the definitive decisions of what are considered to be general church councils. The latter (the ordinary magisterium) includes papal bulls (other than those of the extraordinary magisterium) and encyclicals, and also the unanimous decisions of the councils of bishops.[2]

While there is much to be said in favor of the claim that the church has an obligation to teach — and more generally, to pass on — "the faith which was once delivered unto the saints" (Jude 3), there are several difficulties surrounding the way the magisterium is understood in Roman Catholicism, including, in some cases, exactly where to draw the line between the two kinds of magisterium and also between the ordinary

2. See Francis A. Sullivan, *Magisterium* (Dublin: Gill and MacMillan, 1983), p. 121.

magisterium and statements from the pope or from bishops that are meant to teach, but do not have the full authority of the magisterium.

Let us begin with the three declarations most commonly referred to as infallible teachings.

As we saw in chapter 2, the text of the 1854 bull, *Ineffabilis Deus,* includes the claim that "all human beings [Jesus and Mary excepted] are born infected with original guilt" *(omnes homines nasci originali culpa infectos).* I have argued in earlier chapters that the doctrine of original guilt *(culpa,* or *reatus),* commonly found in the teaching of the Western churches and enshrined in the decrees of the Council of Trent, is fundamentally mistaken — and also unbiblical. On this matter, the teaching of the Orthodox churches that denies the notion of an inherited guilt while accepting a significant sense of both an original sin and of an inherited stain (referring to a universal moral weakness that is both individual and social) is, in my view, closer to biblical teaching and is more in accord with the logic of how we use the word "guilt" in ordinary language, in ethical thinking, and in law. One perhaps paradoxical consequence of this is that, since all human beings are born guiltless, I accept the doctrine of the Immaculate Conception of Mary. In the most fundamental sense, all of us, Mary included, are born "immaculate." However, there is a major problem within the theology of the bull that surrounds the claim concerning Mary. I accept that Mary presents us with a special case of both virtue and of divine grace; but this elevation is undermined if she were born with some special advantage, resulting from a miracle at the time of her conception, as if she were in some way free from the pressures that affect all of us within our state of collective weakness.

In this matter it is interesting to compare the situation of Jesus. The New Testament teaches us that he, too, though without sin, was "tempted in all ways like us" (Heb. 4:15); nevertheless, his situation was different from that of all of us, including Mary. He had (again, according to New Testament teaching) a preexistence, which means that Jesus had a moral character prior to his human birth. This does not imply that Jesus could not also have had a human character that was partially dependent on the environment in which he grew up. However, it seems to me that the moral perfection of Jesus has to be part of any coherent account of his divinity. Moreover, since sin often refers not only to wrong actions but also to the typical human *state,* I think that the church has been correct in denying that Jesus was born with original sin. However, the reason for this claim (i.e., his preexistence) has not, in my view, always been properly understood. In particular, there is no need to link his moral perfection with the doctrine of the virgin birth, as it is in Aquinas.[3]

Given the distinction between original sin (which all except Jesus should be said to have) and original guilt (which Jeremy Taylor and the Orthodox tradition rightly reject), then we have, in *Ineffabilis Deus,* a document of central importance for Catholicism that raises major difficulties for the rational inquirer because of its reliance on an unacceptable — indeed, an irrational — doctrine of original guilt. The notion of inherited guilt (as Abelard saw), in addition to being unbiblical, is in tension with the logic of "guilt." We may recall that Jesus said to the Pharisees, "If you had been blind you would have had no sin" (John 9:41). This succeeds in summing up our ordinary human understanding, that is, that one can only be guilty, in any significant sense of the term, if one is aware that something is wrong and is able to choose otherwise. (Infallibility should not, in fairness, be attributed to every statement in *Ineffabilis Deus,* and that is why I refer to "difficulties" rather than outright contradiction.)

There have been some attempts to distance official teaching from an insistence on inherited guilt by claiming that *culpa,* or *reatus,* does not always mean "guilt" in the modern sense.[4] However, I think that such attempts fail to appreciate the clear meaning of the doctrine in many ancient sources, including the decrees of the Council of Trent.[5] Moving to the 1870 declaration of infallibility, we find a highly controversial claim that was rejected at the time by many Catholic scholars, notably Döllinger, who was excommunicated because of his refusal to accept it.

3. On this matter, see Langford, *Unblind Faith,* chap. 3. Aquinas took the view that our original sin (which, for him, included *reatus,* or *culpa*) is inherited through the semen and hence only through the human father. See *Summa Theologiae* 1a2ae Q81, A4 ad 3; A5 ad 2.

4. We find this in supporters of the Westminster Confession (1646-47) as well as in defenders of traditional Catholicism. See, e.g., J. Tulloch, *The Christian Doctrine of Sin* (Edinburgh: Blackwood, 1876), pp. 192-94, 241-43; see also the sensitivity to the problem of inherited guilt in the article "Original Sin" in the most recent edition of the *New Catholic Encyclopedia* (Washington, DC: Gale, 2003), vol. 10.

5. *Decrees of the Council of Trent,* session 5, June 17, 1546, which speaks of *reatum originalis peccati.*

The only other comment I shall make here is that there are special difficulties with the logic of any pronouncement that refers to itself.

Moving to the 1950 declaration concerning the bodily Assumption of Mary: when this is seen as symbolism, I hold that something interesting and potentially important is being said. Contrary to what is often assumed, the mainstream Christian doctrine of eternal life is not one of a Platonic or Cartesian "soul" eternally existing of its own right, but of an animated spiritual "body" that has some extraordinary continuity with the body we have in this life, and by which we can be recognized as individual persons. (The nature of this continuity presents a classical problem for the philosophy of religion, and my own view is that it can only be provided through a relationship between the individual person and an eternal Mind.) The Assumption of Mary can thus be seen as a kind of symbolic prototype for all of us in which there is a change to a different kind of "body," but a body nonetheless. My two problems with the doctrine are, first, a doubt about whether this represents an actual historical event (because of the total lack of evidence for this outside a church tradition that is much later than the New Testament); and second (more importantly), a difficulty in seeing why this doctrine, even if true, should be given the status of a *de fide* teaching and thus placed alongside — though not necessarily equated with — the doctrines of creation and incarnation as "articles of faith."

With respect to those infallible pronouncements that come from general councils, the Greek Orthodox Church, once again, raises a major issue when it claims that genuinely ecumenical (or universal) church councils have not taken place since the Great Schism between the Eastern and Western Church of 1054 (making the Second Council of Nicaea, in 787 CE, the last truly ecumenical council).[6]

Let us turn to the "ordinary" magisterium. A few examples will suffice to highlight the difficulties. The findings of the Pontifical Biblical Commission in 1902 include the assertions that the apostle Matthew wrote Saint Matthew's Gospel, that the book of Isaiah was written by one person, that Moses wrote the first five books of the Old Testament, ex-

---

6. The traditional date for the Great Schism is 1054, but in fact the schism was a process not marked by any one dramatic event.

cept perhaps the passages dealing with his death, and so on.[7] Very few biblical scholars in any tradition now believe that the commission's claims that I have just listed, along with many others, are acceptable. However, a Vatican decree of 1907, *Praestantia Scripturae,* insisted that all Catholics are bound in conscience to accept the findings of this commission, both of the past and of the future. In addition, the papal encyclical *Veritatis Splendor* (1993) insists that Catholics may not pick and choose between bits of the magisterium: they must treat all parts as though they are infallible (though technically this is not their status in the case of the ordinary magisterium).

With respect to ethics, if we go back into the past, the most infamous case of what — in the language of later times — might properly be called the ordinary magisterium is the official support of torture for heretics in the bull of 1252, *Ad extirpanda,* which underwrote official policy until the end of the eighteenth century. According to this teaching, the church would not itself torture heretics but would hand them over to the secular arm for punishment. More recent examples are the prohibition, in the encyclical *Humanae Vitae* (1968), of the use of condoms, even for married couples, and the claims that the practice of voluntary sterilization (e.g., by husbands who already have several children) is morally wrong, even though — in the case of male vasectomies — such procedures are nearly always reversible.

Teachings such as these have led to an intense debate within Catholicism. That there is the possibility of both factual and moral error (e.g., concerning the authorship of Isaiah and the torture of heretics respectively) is not seriously in doubt, but interesting questions arise concerning how far the ordinary magisterium binds a Catholic person's conscience. Pronouncements such as *Praestantia Scripturae* and *Veritatis Splendor* suggest that the good Catholic is bound to assent, even though they do not claim that it is impossible for the church to be wrong in these matters. In a similar vein, the latest edition of the *New Catholic Encyclo-*

---

7. This commission was set up in 1902, and its conclusions can be found in the Vatican publication *Acta Sanctae Sedis,* followed, after 1909, by the *Acta Apostolicae Sedis.* On Mosaic authorship, see *De Mosaica Authentia Pentateuchi* in the former series (1906), pp. 377-78. The teaching allows some flexibility in terms of glosses to the original text.

pedia (2003) asserts: "It is a common opinion among theologians, however, that ordinary teaching of the magisterium must be accepted, even internally, and obeyed."[8] In contrast, some Catholic theologians allow for reservations respecting both thought and action.[9]

Of course, no Catholic is now expected to follow the teachings of the old bulls, such as *Ad extirpanda* and *Inter caetera* (the 1493 bull of Pope Alexander VI granting Spanish dominion of many parts of South America — without the consent of the aboriginal people). Although they have not been formally repealed, to the best of my knowledge, more recent teachings have completely changed what is considered right in matters such as the persecution of heretics and the occupation of aboriginal lands. In fact, since the publication of *Rerum Novarum* in 1891, the social teaching of the Roman Catholic Church has been generally progressive. Nevertheless, I would hold that there is something profoundly unsatisfactory in the very existence of these old bulls, because the fact that the church could get things so wrong in the past may understandably make us nervous about whether it has gotten everything right in the present, and may make us wonder about the nature of the "authority" that the church should be accorded.

Within this very complex set of theological and moral issues, it can be argued that there is a difference between the person who is born a Roman Catholic and one who chooses to become one. Many of those who are born into the faith say something like this: "I have been born a Catholic, and although I do not agree with some parts of mainstream Catholic teaching [including parts of the ordinary magisterium, and in the case of some of my acquaintances who call themselves Catholic, parts of the extraordinary magisterium as well] I do not see any need to abandon a faith in which I find much consolation. I don't agree with the church's position on, say, contraception, or the refusal to ordain women, or celibacy, but I have never, as it were, 'signed up' to such teachings."[10] I personally know many

8. *New Catholic Encyclopedia*, 13:247.

9. See Sullivan, *Magisterium*, pp. 169-73.

10. Strictly speaking, the celibacy issue is not theological; rather, it is a matter of church discipline. It is generally agreed that the majority of Catholic priests were married prior to the twelfth century, and the subsequent ban on the marriage of priests was not, at least primarily, based on a theological principle.

devout Roman Catholics who would have little, if any, difficulty agreeing with almost everything I have written in this book. I have much sympathy with these people, and I believe that their position is in some ways different from those who choose to become Catholic even though they clearly disagree with parts of the recent magisterium. For most people, it would seem that the decision to become a Catholic involves, among other things, a public acceptance of the magisterium, at least with respect to formal teachings made within the last few decades. When that is not the case, I have a problem understanding the act of becoming a Catholic.

I would be the first to admit that liberals also have a problem with authority, namely, the very different problem that they are sometimes unsure exactly what they should believe. In addition, there is a tendency toward vagueness of doctrine in many followers of a liberal path. But I believe that these are lesser evils. The wrong kind of certainty has bedeviled Christian history and been the source of huge amounts of persecution and suffering. Richard Hooker's rejection of "certainty of evidence" and Sebastian Castellio's "art of doubting" provide, I suggest, a preferable path. It is also a path that is perfectly consistent with the character and teachings of Jesus, who, when he was asked a question, typically responded not with an authoritative statement but with either another question to take home and ponder or a parable that required serious reflection. More importantly, this lack of intellectual certainty can go hand in hand with a positive commitment to be a genuine disciple of Jesus.

The magisterium presents other difficulties. Take, for example, the declaration of Pope Pius XII, in his Christmas message of 1956, that Catholics should not invoke their private consciences in order to refuse conscription, provided that a declaration of war is made by a democratic government. This implies that all those American Catholics who, as a matter of conscience, refused to fight in Vietnam acted wrongly. I prefer the position of Richard Baxter on the hugely significant issue of going to war, where even private soldiers have some duty of reflection.[11] When the wrongness of a war is clearly evident to a citizen, it would seem that disobedience to the sovereign or magistrate is right; but in cases of doubt the

11. Richard Baxter, *A Christian Directory* (incorporating *Cases of Conscience*) (London, 1673), 4:46-47; see also p. 187.

discussion becomes complex, and the implication is that sometimes the citizen should obey. Personally, I would take a stronger line on doubtful cases, bearing in mind how often soldiers have been commanded to fight in unjust wars, even under relatively democratic regimes.

Consider also Pope John Paul II's declaration, on March 20, 2004, that artificial hydration (e.g., by a nasograstric tube) is part of "normal" care for the sick and may not be discontinued even if such is the request of a competent patient nearing death. Like many other papal decisions, these declarations, though clearly not presented as infallible, are official papal pronouncements that are, in some sense, part of the contemporary magisterium. They are simultaneously a source of major disagreement, even among Catholics.[12]

C. Dialectical Theology

Strictly speaking, the third Christian position that I want to contrast with liberal theology should not be referred to as a conservative form of Christianity but as "dialectical theology," or "neo-orthodoxy." Nevertheless, it has sufficient similarities to how many people use the word "conservative" to warrant being discussed here. My suggestion is not so much that it is totally wrong as that it overemphasizes certain truths at the expense of others. The tradition I am referring to is best exemplified by the writings of Karl Barth (1886-1968), and his supporters will almost certainly say, with some justification, that my brief summary of his position is incomplete.

Barth first developed his position while opposing the war policies of Kaiser Wilhelm II, and subsequently while opposing Nazism, following his expulsion from Germany in 1935. Consequently, it is often claimed that the stark contrasts he draws between the absolute demands of the gospel and the evils of the world have to be appreciated in this context, a context in which an extraordinarily brutal form of evil (under Adolf Hitler) was stalking the world — to which the Christian gospel was indeed a polar opposite.

---

12. For a Catholic response to the 2004 papal address, see *Health Ethics Today* 14, no. 2 (2004), John Dossetor Health Centre, University of Alberta, Edmonton.

According to Barth, God speaks to us, uniquely, in Jesus Christ, and his voice cannot be subjected to any form of human judgment. As dialectical theology is often expressed, God's word comes to us vertically (from on high) and not horizontally (as mediated through human sources). Only in Jesus Christ is the divine activity revealed to us. Thus arises Barth's dismissal of all "natural theology," that is, of the ancient tradition according to which human reason can begin to ascend to some divine matters, for example, in Aquinas's arguments for the existence and basic nature of God.

Barth makes an equivalent challenge to many forms of traditional Christian ethics, especially in the natural law tradition, according to which human reason can begin to discern a universal moral law that is applicable to all human beings. Barth does allow a certain place for ethical books and lectures, "treated independently, that is, in external separation from dogmatics, so long as it is presupposed that this separation is understood and treated as purely technical, and thus that dogmatics is not detached from its ethical content and direction and that the question of dogmatics remains paramount and decisive in ethics."[13] This means, in effect, that according to Barth, the ethical demands of the gospel must trump traditional arguments based on various forms of moral philosophy. On this basis, some writers who are sympathetic to Barth take a stand on practical issues such as abortion and euthanasia.[14] With respect to these, it is argued, a "Christian anthropology," rooted in the biblical view of both creation and redemption, demands a powerful statement of what is right that cannot be countered by the arguments typically used equally by secular humanists and liberal Christians, for example, about universal human rights.[15]

13. Karl Barth, *Church Dogmatics*, III/4, ed. G. W. Bromiley and T. F. Torrance, trans. A. T. Mackay et al. (Edinburgh: T&T Clark, 1961), §52, pp. 3-4.

14. In his detailed discussion of abortion, Barth defends the view that the infant should be regarded as a human being from the beginning, but he also criticizes the Roman Catholic position for placing the value of the child's life above that of the mother. As a result, his position does allow for some rare exceptions and is not "absolutist" in the strict sense. See Barth, *Church Dogmatics*, III/4, §55, p. 415.

15. Ethics is Christian, e.g., "in so far as it is dogmatic — that is, in so far as it allows its form and content to be shaped by, and tested against, the affirmations of Christian

It is often pointed out that, though Barth argues strenuously against both natural theology and (an independent) philosophical ethics, his writings, especially in later years, do in practice make some accommodations to both, through a genuine sensitivity to the need to engage in rational discussion with others. For example, during his discussion of capital punishment he makes a sympathetic reference to the Enlightenment thinker Beccaria.[16] As it is sometimes put, rational considerations tend to creep in by the back door, as it were

The basis of my response to Barthianism is to be found in my agreement with Aquinas's refrain that the order of divine grace does not destroy nature but rather fulfills or completes it *(gratia non tollat naturam sed perficiat).*[17] When this position is emphasized, the gospel message is not so much a divine no to human strivings as it is a yes to all those strivings that reflect a God-given awareness of what is good or true or beautiful. In the light of this, other religious traditions — and indeed certain aspects of secular humanism — can be seen as positive attempts to respond to the divine *Logos.* Christianity still has something unique to say, but it is a message that completes and fulfills human endeavors, taken at their best, rather than a denial of them. This is one reason why William Chillingworth is such a key figure in what I have called the liberal tradition.

Key to this liberal response to Barthianism is the way the words recorded in John's Gospel ("no-one comes to the Father except through me," 14:6) are interpreted. As we have seen (e.g., in the comments on Origen and Chillingworth in chap. 3 above), it is perfectly possible to interpret these words in a liberal way. In this view, the "me" is the eternal *Logos,* God's "Word" to human beings as it comes to them within their

---

doctrine" (Michael Banner, *Christian Ethics and Contemporary Moral Problems* [Cambridge, UK: Cambridge University Press, 1999], p. 269). I was tempted to refer to an "absolutist" position on ethical issues, but Banner argues that "absolutism" is an inappropriate and misleading term for the kind of position he advocates. See Michael Banner, *The Practice of Abortion* (London: Darton, Longman and Todd, 1999), pp. 16-17.

16. Barth, *Church Dogmatics,* vol. 3, part 4, para. 55, p. 438, argues that capital punishment is wrong and severely criticizes both Catholic and Protestant traditions on this matter. However, as in his discussion of abortion, he does allow some rare exceptions, in this case where a state is in such a dangerous situation that its survival depends on adopting measures that would not normally be justified.

17. Aquinas, *Summa Theologiae,* 1a, Q1, A8, *ad* 2. Similar expressions occur elsewhere.

own language and culture. What is unique about Christianity is the belief that this Word was also incarnate in a particular and historical human life. Many insights follow from this belief, but they do not have to include the negative assessment of natural theology and natural law referred to above.

Similar remarks apply to the notion of divine transcendence. Barth, like many of those who are worried by what has been presented as liberal theology, is rightly eager to preserve an understanding of the nature of God that does not diminish his stature by framing him in purely human terms. I have tried to argue that the divine transcendence is not under threat from liberal theology when the latter is properly presented. It only appears to be so for two reasons: first, some of those *called* liberals have departed from the kind of mainstream Christianity that accepts the Apostles' Creed (albeit with a certain latitude in interpretation) and have produced a caricature of the liberal tradition that I have tried to give an account of here; second, the claim that human thought at its best can attain some glimmerings of a real understanding of the divine (a kind of limited natural theology) is properly rooted, not in a denial of transcendence, but in an alternative, Christian account of creation. In this account, the Creator has chosen to leave a stamp or image of himself within humankind, a kind of "candle of the Lord" within us that enables us, within certain limits, to transcend the purely natural order.[18] According to this view (which is that of Thomas Aquinas), though the *apophatic* (or negative) way may often be emphasized, in which we can only truthfully say what God is not, there is also room for a limited *cataphatic* (or positive) way. This "positive way" has at least two aspects. First, it means that some analogies for the nature of God can be found in human experience, because this is how the transcendent has chosen to make us. Second, it means that the human capacity to reason is itself a kind of divine gift in which, in the language of Aquinas, we can begin to "participate" in the eternal law of God.[19] This view allows us to claim that some philoso-

18. The expression "the candle of the Lord" was used by some of the Cambridge Platonists, particularly Nathaniel Culverwell, to refer to the kind of rational capacity with which humans have been endowed by the Creator.

19. One powerful example of this is Aquinas's definition of natural law: *participatio legis aeternae in rationali creatura "lex naturae" dicitur (S.T.* 1a2ae, Q91, A2).

phers, such as Plato, as well as some non-Christian religions, may have something to teach us. For Barthians there is a danger that preaching can take over from serious dialogue with non-Christians; for liberals, by contrast, there is more optimism about the results of a dialogue in which it is accepted that the non-Christian party may also be open to the promptings of the *Logos*. Liberal theology has much greater grounds for hope regarding such dialogue, and its optimism need not be founded on a denial of transcendence but on a different view of the divine creation.

This disagreement with Barth has implications for ethics, as I shall illustrate in two ways. First, there are his statements concerning the Jewish invasion of Palestine under Joshua. I have noted (in chapter 3) how Hannah Barnard, at the end of the eighteenth century, argued that the massacres committed by the invading Israelites were not what God had commanded, but what they *thought* God had commanded. We also observed that much earlier, Origen, who was sensitive to the apparent injustice of God in these stories, insisted in his *Homilies on Joshua* that their real meaning concerned the overcoming of vices within our hearts. Without interpretations along these lines, it is difficult to make sense of the crucial claim "God is good." In his *Dogmatics*, Barth does not discuss these massacres except to refer to the "destruction" of many of the original inhabitants of Palestine; but in an illuminating passage he does discuss the invasion of Palestine, and he uses it as a prime example of how philosophical ethics is negated by divine ethics.[20] "From the point of view of the general history of ethics, it [that is, 'the command of God and the revelation of the good which takes place in it'] means an annexation of the kind that took place on the entry of the children of Israel into Palestine. Other people had for a long time maintained that they had a very old, if not the oldest, right of domicile in this country. But, according to Joshua 9:27, they could now at best exist only as 'hewers of wood and drawers of water.'"[21]

Even if one extracts the massacres from this scene of "annexation," the picture of God's justice presented in this approach is worrisome, and

---

20. E.g., Barth, *Church Dogmatics*, II/2, ed. G. W. Bromiley and T. F. Torrance (Edinburgh: T&T Clark, 1957), §35, p. 356.

21. Barth, *Church Dogmatics*, II/2, §36, pp. 518-19.

dare I say, of a piece with the apparently different, Catholic tradition that could view God as sanctioning — perhaps commanding — the torture of heretics (in the *Ad extirpanda* of 1252). Centuries of peaceful occupation apparently give one no right of ownership over against an invading and cruel enemy, who may (quite properly) enslave you, if this is in accordance with God's command. Here we revisit a theme of central importance for the tradition of liberal theology that I raised in chapter 2 (in the discussion of the relationship of reason to revelation) and chapter 3 (seen in the contrasting positions of Hannah Barnard and Kierkegaard). If "good" is defined purely in terms of what God tells us is good (either in a literal reading of Scripture or through some of the former claims made by a Catholic magisterium), then the hugely important claim "God is good" is in danger of being totally emasculated. (This is what is called the *euthyphro* question in the history of philosophy.)

Furthermore, the issue before us is not just one of historical importance — for at least two reasons. First, it is not by chance that a large number of conservative, often "born-again," Christians in the United States have formally approved the systematic torture (e.g., via waterboarding) of both terrorists and terrorist suspects. Respect for the transcendence of God, made in opposition to humanistic ethics, all too easily becomes a way of interpreting certain biblical passages in an absolutist way, consequently turning a blind eye to human rules, such as those of the Geneva Conventions. There is a paradox here, because Barth, to his credit, was appalled by equivalent atrocities, and yet he has championed a theology that can lead to an approval of them (despite his undoubted rejection of such interpretations) — whether in Joshua or Guantanamo Bay. In contrast to the kind of certainty with which conservatives of many hues interpret Scripture, I prefer the distrust of certainty that we have seen in the sections on Castellio and Hooker. Second, there is the contemporary question of the right of Jewish settlers to Palestinian lands, both in the West Bank and within the actual borders of Israel, from which some three quarters of a million fearful Arabs fled in 1948.[22] Barth's comments on the book of Joshua could easily be used

---

22. On this matter, see Ilan Pappe, *The Ethnic Cleansing of Palestine* (Oxford: One World, 2006).

to support a brutal and illegal (under international law) occupation of Palestinian lands.

I must, of course, consider the most obvious and immediate response to my challenge. If God is indeed God and the Creator ex nihilo, he cannot be judged by human standards; rather, what we call the "good" must somehow be grounded in him. However, my argument does not amount to a denial of this claim. To understand how this can be true, let us remember an insufficiently familiar distinction that Aquinas makes between what he calls the *via inventionis* and the *via judicii*.[23] My suggestion (which is, I believe, a legitimate expansion of Aquinas's distinction) goes as follows: According to the former (the way of discovery), we come to know that God is good through a human process in which we first learn something of the substantive meaning of good through human experience, particularly through the kinds of cooperative activities that make human, communal existence possible, especially if it is to flourish.[24] When, subsequent to this, we read in prophets like Isaiah about God's concern with justice, and later about his concern with love, we (or perhaps, more accurately, the first hearers of Isaiah) come to *discover* that God is indeed good. However, once we have discovered both this initial meaning of "good," and that God *is* good (through a *via inventionis*), a deeper understanding (or *via judicii*) can begin to develop. Two things happen. First, what we initially thought of as good is corrected and enlarged (but not totally contradicted) in the light of God's word. This does not mean that philosophers like Plato had it all wrong but that, once again, grace has fulfilled nature. Second, we realize not only that God is good but that creation is such that God could not be other than good — indeed, "the Good." None of this, however, reduces the extraordinary force of the human *discovery* that "God is good" (implicit, e.g., in Isa.

---

23. Aquinas, *Summa Theologiae*, e.g., 1a, Q79, A8-9. Gordon Kaufman makes use of a similar (but not identical) distinction between the "order of knowing" and the "order of being" in *An Essay on Theological Method*, rev. ed. (Ann Arbor, MI: Scholars Press, 1979), p. 4.

24. Linguistic philosophers have argued that the most basic meaning of "good" is that of the most general word for commendation. However, I am here concerned with the more subtle question of what things, if any, are substantively good. These, I suggest, must include a measure of reciprocity, because this is a precondition of human flourishing.

6:16). This point has a meaning of quite extraordinary importance, because when we make this point, there is not only a no to the cruelties, for example, of the Roman amphitheater, but a yes to the affirmation of God as the one who fulfills as well as transcends the noblest of human strivings.

There is an interesting parallel between the way God must be the Good (even though our first acquaintance with "good" does not come from revelation but from human, communal living) and the way God — if he is to be God — must exist "necessarily" (even though the ontological argument is not for us, strictly speaking, valid).[25] Once again, I follow Aquinas here. If we could see God's nature for what it is, then we would be able to affirm the conclusion of the ontological argument with certainty; but we cannot do so from within our present condition (pace Anselm). Just as (from the perspective of the *via judicii*) God must be "He who is," so from the same perspective he must be "the Good." However, absolute certainties, in both cases, demand a going beyond the *via inventionis* that is not possible in this life. The *via judicii*, I would suggest, is something that practicing Christians begin to enter into here, but only imperfectly.

There is an analogy for this situation within music. When well performed, some of Bach's works combine a sense of inevitability, especially if the piece is well known ("this is how the pattern must work out") with, paradoxically, a sense of repeated surprise, so that the piece is forever fresh and full of wonder! This, I suggest, parallels the way in which the sense of discovery, as in the *via inventionis*, is matched by a sense of entering a timeless truth, and a kind of inevitability — as in the *via judicii*.

My second illustration concerns Barth's treatment of homosexuality.[26] He believes that all homosexual practice is ruled out by "the command of God," and the current situation indicates what happens "when man refuses to admit the validity of the divine command." There are two main problems here. The first echoes the earlier discussion and the need

25. Anselm's ontological argument claimed that we can see that God must exist necessarily once we have grasped the concept of God as the being, a greater than whom cannot be conceived. Aquinas identified the problem as our inability fully to grasp the meaning of this concept, at least in this life.

26. Barth, *Church Dogmatics*, III/4, §54, p. 166.

for a Christian philosophy that makes the claim that "God is good" coherent. In Aquinas there are crucial distinctions between (1) natural law (which is his equivalent to both the universal natural justice of Aristotle and the universal moral law of Paul in Romans 2:15); (2) positive divine law (when something is morally enjoined simply because it is commanded by God, typically as in the ceremonial law of the Old Testament, but, more generally, in any sense of a vocation); (3) human law (the equivalent to the *ius civile* of Roman law). In the light of positive divine law (2 above), if we accept Barth's claim that all homosexual activity is forbidden by God, this would provide a moral reason for Christians (and perhaps other monotheists, depending on the nature of the divine authority they accept) to forbid it for their community; but it would not, by itself, provide a reason for others.

However, traditional Christians have clearly not claimed that homosexuality was only wrong for them (or for others within the biblical tradition); they have claimed that there is some universal moral requirement regarding homosexuality. In other words, they have claimed that the prohibition is part of a universal moral law, and *not only* part of positive divine law. In the case of many other moral commands, it is easy to see how the argument can be extended to allow this. For example, the prohibition of murder is not only part of the Ten Commandments; it is an obvious necessity for any communal and peaceful community. For this reason Aquinas argued that the moral commands of the Decalogue, though part of positive divine law in that they are commanded by God, are *in themselves* part of a natural or universal moral law that has been given, as it were, the added sanction of divine command. Even in the case of the fourth commandment, there are plausible arguments for saying that one day in seven should be reserved for rest.[27] However, if a reason cannot be given for a moral command that "makes sense" to human beings who do not share the biblical tradition, then the situation is very unsatisfactory: a universal moral injunction is invoked that is only based on a particular religious tradition. Such a tradition, I repeat, may

27. In Canada, when there were proposals to remove restrictions on hunting on Sundays, the chorus of opposition included the voices of many secular people who wanted at least one day in the week when they could walk in the woods without being shot at by trigger-happy hunters.

be adequate for a positive divine law but not for a universal, or "natural," moral law.

In recognition of this requirement, there have been, of course, many attempts to argue (using "general arguments") that all homosexuality is wrong, and many of these have come from writers within the natural-law tradition. However, these arguments have problems.[28] (I am not referring to arguments against the sexual abuse of minors, or of other vulnerable people, nor those against promiscuity — for all of which there are clear, universal moral arguments that apply equally to heterosexual and homosexual relationships. I am concerned here only with monogamous relationships between consenting adults, especially among those who find, perhaps as a result of genetic disposition, that "this is the way they have been made.")

The second main problem is the claim that some biblical passages do actually prove that there is a universal and divine prohibition on homosexual activity. I accept that God does have a right to make commands that should be treated by us as absolute, even if they go beyond any universal (natural) law, as in the case of a vocation; but the problem comes in determining that something is, in fact, such a command. Clearly, reliance on Old Testament law is very unsatisfactory, partly because many of the moral laws seem very hard to disentangle from ritual laws (e.g., the provision that an animal used in bestiality should be killed [Exod. 2:19][29]), and partly because Jesus rejected at least some of this law

28. These arguments often depend on the alleged "purpose" of sex, namely, survival of the species. However, even within the framework of biology, it is by no means certain that reproduction is the only purpose. For scientific data on these topics, see chap. 2 above, notes 56 and 57. If, in response, it is claimed that — from a strictly biological point of view — my argument still leaves procreation as the only "ultimate" *telos* of sex, I would point out that even within the papal encyclical *Humanae Vitae* (1968), procreation is not the only *moral* function of coition, for the use of sex to cement the marriage relationship is permitted even if there is no possibility of procreation, e.g., because of the age of the woman. (There is the proviso that there must be no intention to prevent procreation except, perhaps inconsistently, with the deliberate use of the "rhythm method.")

29. This verse illustrates the difficulties well. There is indeed a moral case for punishing the human person involved in bestiality because there is likely to be either cruelty or unnecessary indignity shown to the animal, but — ritual uncleanness aside — it

("an eye for an eye and a tooth for a tooth"). Barth relies on Romans 1, but this is only a little more satisfactory, for while a command from Jesus would indeed be finally authoritative for any mainstream Christian, it is not clear that an opinion of Paul should be regarded in the same way.[30] His disapproval of much Roman practice, including the sexual exploitation of slaves, is easily supported by what I have called "general arguments"; but if Paul meant to condemn all kinds of homosexual practice, which I think is probable, then, when we are faced with the equivalent of monogamous relationships in which both love and commitment are

---

is hard to see why the animal should pay a penalty. Most of the time we can fairly easily make such a distinction between the moral and the ritual, but I doubt whether the situation was anything like as clear-cut in the minds of the people to whom Exodus and Leviticus were first addressed. However, in the decisions of the Council of Jerusalem (c. 50 CE, in Acts 15) the distinction is evident.

30. The appearance of such a command would raise some difficult questions. First, how sure could we be that there was an actual dominical command and not an interpolation by the early church? If the genuineness were to be established, the next question would be: "Is this part of positive divine law, or part of universal moral law?" If the former, then, in my view, Christians should simply accept it as part of their vocation; but if the latter, a new set of questions would arise. These would parallel the way in which moral decisions of the Vatican are often couched in natural-law language, with the implication that what is enjoined is "really" in accord with reason and is not based purely on authority. This harks back to the Stoic concept of *recta ratio*, which, while claiming the title of "reason," in fact relied on a particular form of intuitional reason that only the enlightened possess. (In the language of the Stoics, those whose individual sparks of fire were properly absorbed into the great Fire would be so enlightened.) This is paralleled, I am suggesting, in the *Humanae Vitae*, when the final encyclical was based on the minority report of only four of the fifty-five Catholic experts who were originally appointed, the other fifty-one having written a dissenting opinion based on their understanding of natural law.

A defense of the "this is really rational" approach can be mounted along these lines: A poor mathematician, faced with a good mathematician who was trying to explain, say, one of Einstein's 1905 papers, might conclude "I just cannot follow this, but I accept that you, as an expert, can tell me what is proved." However, we apply this analogy to moral reasoning at our peril, because in the Einstein case all seriously qualified mathematicians might agree, while in moral matters (as in the example of the fifty-five Catholic experts) they manifestly do not. Perhaps it is better to put the matter this way: In mathematics and many other disciplines there are clear criteria for being an "expert," criteria that do not apply in the context of morality. In sum, even a dominical command that was *claimed* to be a reference to universal morality would seem to require some kind of "reasoning" that "makes sense" to the ordinary person.

manifest, further argument is necessary.[31] A simple appeal to an alleged divine command is not sufficient.

I do not want to be misunderstood here. I am not claiming that all those who adopt what I have called liberal theology will also adopt what might be referred to as a "liberal agenda" in ethics. (Personally, I have considerable reservations regarding what is sometimes included in this agenda.) Moreover, there are good grounds for insisting that a Christian ethics must take into account the central doctrines of creation, the Fall, and redemption. Indeed, one of the problems with many presentations of what is alleged to be "Christian ethics" is that they do not show why the adjective "Christian" is applicable. However, I hold that it is possible to do this in a way that is consistent with Aquinas's approach, in which our understanding of grace completes and enriches a more general understanding that human beings can acquire.[32]

31. Some scholars have interpreted Paul to refer only to exploitative sex. Given the Jewish tradition in which Paul grew up I think it more probable that he did indeed intend to condemn all homosexual activity. Consequently I do not want to rely on this questionable interpretation in order to avoid the difficulties posed by Rom. 1.

32. In my view, the principal way in which Christian ethics is different from that of secular humanism is that although similar (possibly identical) moral principles are often supported, Christian ethics can "ground" these much more adequately. E.g., Kant's formulation of the categorical imperative, "Treat every person as an end in themselves and not as a mere means," is common ground for Christians and many atheists, but I would argue that a grounding in a doctrine of creation and redemption makes it both more intelligible and more powerful. Moreover, there are situations where the *content* of ethics can be affected (or effected) by Christian belief. For example, a secular utilitarian might plausibly argue that a world in which everyone died in a nuclear holocaust was better than a world in which Stalin and company ruled the whole planet, possibly in perpetuity. (For a utilitarian zero overall human happiness is preferable to any minus number.) Quite apart from a series of philosophical problems with utilitarianism, a Christian who believes in grace could never accept this justification for all-out nuclear warfare. Whatever the human predictions, belief in grace would hold that — as in the Babylonian captivity — God will bring good out of evil; also that, in any case, we have no right to destroy the divine creation. Many secularists, of course, would agree that there could be no adequate justification of an all-out nuclear war, but they could not rely on arguments about grace or creation. Issues remain about how far Christian ethics is different from other forms of theistic ethics that also have a concept of grace. Here, I would argue, the *content* of ethics is still more similar than in the case of a secular humanist, but there still needs to be an exploration of how far specifically

D. Materialism

In this section I am once again putting together many belief systems that a longer treatment would need to distinguish. However, my particular target is the form of secular humanism that is positively opposed to religious belief in all its forms. It is not so much *agnostic* (meaning simply that one "does not know") as it is *atheist* (meaning that one is positively denying that there is a God). When the word "agnostic" is used in its strict sense, some Christians call themselves agnostic: that is, they claim to believe rather than to know. Leslie Weatherhead was an inspirational Methodist preacher and writer who took this position. In popular usage, however, the word "agnostic" usually refers to someone who neither knows nor believes.

In many cases, the position adopted by atheists is more "dogmatic" than my own. I have suggested all along that although atheism is in my view mistaken, it is a perfectly plausible position for an intelligent person to take. This is not to say, however, that all — or even most — atheists are in fact rational, given the account of rationality that I have provided in chapter 2. But, to repeat an earlier refrain, both theism and atheism (along with some other possibilities, such as monism and logical positivism) can, at their best, represent rational systems of belief.[33] Similarly, I am not claiming that the overall positions of many Christians

---

Christian doctrines, such as those of the Trinity, the Fall, and atonement, affect (or effect) either the status or the content of ethics. (In the foregoing discussion I need to emphasize the term "all-out" because the issue of whether or not nuclear weapons could justifiably be used in certain tactical situations requires a more extended analysis. I am referring to the use of weapons in situations in which the survival of our species would be in peril.)

33. Logical positivists, such as A. J. Ayer, deny that they are atheists because they say that the concept of God is literally meaningless. Atheism, according to them, suggests that one is denying the existence of x when it is known, at least roughly, what x is. Ayer's original position has been criticized by many philosophers because (among other reasons) of his emphasis on verification when, it has been alleged, it is falsification that is more important for literal meaning. I have some doubts as to whether the kind of logical positivism proposed by Ayer in his *Language, Truth and Logic* (1936) can now be held to be rational, but I accept that an updated version of his argument — that words like "God" are literally meaningless — is plausible, and this is what I refer to here.

or supporters of other major religions are rational, only that there are rational forms of Christianity — as well as of the other major religions.

The reason for this claim about the fundamental irrationality of many atheists is that they tend to depend on two particular fallacies. If they do not depend on these fallacies, I accept that they may be rational, even though I happen to believe that they are mistaken. Elsewhere I have elaborated on two other fallacies in the writings of Richard Dawkins.[34]

(1) The first fallacy begins by pointing out the evil things that have frequently been associated with religious belief and then suggesting that the existence of these evils removes any possibility of a rational belief in a God who is both good and omnipotent. The argument goes back to Epicurus and perhaps before, and it has resurfaced many times, for example, in the writings of Richard Dawkins. This basic false reasoning can be exposed by recalling the old proverb *corruptio optimi pessima* ("the corruption of the best is the worst"). Let us suppose, for the sake of argument, that Dawkins and company are right about the baleful influence of religion. This might show that all traditional forms of religion are bad or mistaken, but logically it would leave quite untouched the truth claim that there is a God — or some other form of spiritual reality. If it is true that the spiritual side of humankind is the most important, then it is quite rational to suppose that its corruption is worse than its absence. In other words, it could be utterly rational to believe that bad religion is much worse than no religion, but this would in no way deny that true religion, if it could be found to be practiced, would be better still. Some atheists actually imply this when they contrast, quite rightly, the character of Jesus himself with that of many of his followers.

34. See Langford, *Unblind Faith*, 2nd ed., chap. 14. These concern (a) the claim that the goodness of God is a kind of "add-on" — when Christianity has always identified God with "the Good," and (b) the claim that the church's choice of the four Gospels was more or less arbitrary, which totally ignores the massive scholarly evidence for the early date of the four canonical Gospels and the much later date of the apocryphal gospels, with the possible exception of the Gospel of Thomas. In sum, the four traditional Gospels were chosen because there was good evidence that they were "apostolic" in that they were written during the apostolic period, and either by eyewitnesses or by those who spoke to eyewitnesses.

In fact, I do not accept the claim that the overall influence of religion has been so uniformly bad. There are certainly terrible episodes, such as the Crusades, the Inquisition, and the boiling alive of Sikhs who refused to accept Islam, in which bad religion played a major role in producing harm; but it is very difficult to make a fair balance between all these negative factors and the positive ones. As examples, consider the positive influence of Christianity on the music of J. S. Bach, who claimed to be writing for the glory of God; or, somewhat later, the Quakers, who spearheaded the abolition of slavery; or, more recently, church initiatives in establishing the hospice movement. As to the claim itself, several points need to be emphasized.

(a) The first concerns the meaning of "omnipotence," and here I revisit a theme from chapter 2. When that term is defined in an absolutist way, namely, as the assertion that God can do anything, there is an immediate ambiguity. This is because mainstream Christians do not assert that God can do literally anything: he cannot, for example, do things that are logically impossible, such as make two plus two equal five (provided we maintain the standard meaning of the terms). Originally, references to God's omnipotence were not to a philosophical doctrine; they were simply expressions of belief in God as the "great, creative power." Philosophical distinctions were not in the minds of the people who first used such language. Much later, when it comes to the philosophical exploration of omnipotence, Aquinas says that not only does it make no sense to say that God could break the law of noncontradiction (what we would now call a logical absurdity); it also makes no sense to speak of him being able to do evil things, because God — by necessity — is the Good. Moreover, God's will is, in an interesting way, subject to (his own) eternal law.[35]

---

35. Aquinas, *Summa Theologiae*, 1a, Q25, A3-4 and 1a 2ae, Q93, A4. We need to use care in the way we express this insight. We have seen that Aquinas prefers to say that it is more appropriate *(convenientius)* to claim that it makes no sense to speak of God's doing evil or breaking the law of noncontradiction than to say that he is "limited" by them. Similarly, the way God is "limited" by his own eternal law needs to be expressed carefully. Although Aquinas writes *voluntas Dei subditur legi aeternae* in 1a 2ae, Q93, A4, this sentence occurs in the opening, explorative section, whereas when he gives his own considered view (beginning with *Responsio*), he writes: *lex aeterna est ratio divinae gubernationis* (rendered in the Gilby edition as "the Eternal Law is the shaping idea in divine government").

Once we realize that Christians do not claim that God is omnipotent in the way many atheists think they claim, many things follow. For example, God cannot *make* people good, because if he did so, they would not be humans — for whom a degree of radical freedom is part of their very nature. Nor, I suggest, could he make a world in which no suffering ever occurred within a world in which people are free to make real choices, and in which the laws of physics apply (which provide a stable world in which outcomes are generally predictable and which thus makes it possible for people to act in a loving and responsible way).[36]

(b) The admitted baleful effects of bad religion must be placed alongside the baleful effects of many atheistic philosophies, such as those of Stalin's version of communism and Hitler's version of fascism. (Hitler sometimes referred to "God," but it was for political reasons, not because he was a true believer.) These are two of many examples in the twentieth century, the first century in which atheism became commonplace. In the light of such evils, it seems simply perverse to lay all evil at the door of religion. Moreover, when it is claimed — as it sometimes is — that Marxism and fascism are really examples of "religion," a new kind of logical confusion enters the scene. It is perfectly true that both of them did introduce some of the trappings usually associated with religion, such as rituals and initiation cults. But another aspect of fallacious reasoning appears when religion is defined in a negative way, while secular humanism (which sometimes also borrows a number of religious trappings, such as codes of conduct, affirmations of values, and powerful oratory) is declared *not* to be a religion and effectively defined in a positive way. In sum, a nonpartisan look at human evil and suffering may well put some of it down to religion (or bad religion), but it will also put it down to many other factors. As to the overall balance between the good and the bad effects of religion, it will probably be very unsure.

(c) Historical and political commentators have increasingly come to see how religious movements are frequently tied in to political and economic movements, so that it is often impossible to tell how much the true causes of a war, or of some other disaster, can be attributed to reli-

36. On this matter, see a more extended treatment in Langford, *Unblind Faith,* 2nd. ed., chap. 10.

gion itself and how much to other factors that ride on the coattails of religion. The British civil war of 1642-49 is sometimes described as a religious war; but it was much more an economic and political war between,
on the one side, most of the gentry class (aided by a growing independent middle class) and, on the other, the royalists, who were supported
not only by most of the aristocracy but also by many of the peasants, who
had no love for the gentry whom they served. Religious differences were
used, but they were not the principal source of the conflict. The same applies to Northern Ireland, where the principal cause of conflict was a
form of colonialism, coupled with oppression and poverty; again, religion became a focus that was an easy way of identifying those on the
other side. The situation in Northern Ireland has some similarities to
that of the Basque area of Spain, where a conquering power has ruled a
body of people that are significantly different in terms of ethnicity, language, and culture. However, because both sides of the conflict are Catholic, this is not referred to as a "religious war." The implication is that if,
in Ireland, there had been no religious difference between the governing
power and the oppressed, the situation, including the acts of terrorism,
might not have been very different. (Indeed, the oppression began with
Norman conquerors, who shared Catholicism with the native people.)
Even the notorious Thirty Years' War (1618-48) was much more complex
than a mere Catholic-Protestant fight. Recent scholarship has highlighted how often Catholics and Protestants were fighting on the same
side in a war that had more political than religious dimensions. "The last
thirteen years of the war — the bloodiest — were essentially a struggle
between the Habsburgs and the Bourbons, the two great Catholic dynas-
ties of Europe."[37] Even in the case of the slaughters at the time of the par-
tition of India, it is difficult to disentangle the religious tensions from
disputes about race, caste, language, natural resources, and political am-
bitions. For centuries, in many parts of imperial India, Muslims, Sikhs,
and Hindus had lived side by side in relative harmony, and one has to
wonder how far the separatist movements that developed suited some of

37. William T. Cavanaugh, "'A Fire Strong Enough to Consume the House': The
Wars of Religion and the Rise of the State," *Modern Theology* 11, no. 4 (Blackwell, October
1995): 403.

the politicians who, rejecting Gandhi's call for a united country, had their own power agendas.

(2) The second major fallacy evident in much atheist writing is the treatment of the fundamental issue as if belief in God were an *empirical* hypothesis. There is a sense in which those who wonder whether or not God is a reality might reasonably treat the question of God's existence as a kind of hypothesis. They might, for example, try living as Christians, as far as possible attempting to think and feel *as if* the essential beliefs were true. At the same time, they might attempt a kind of prayer, beginning always, "Oh God, if you are there. . . ."[38] Within the context of such an "experiment," they might hope that experience had some relevance to the decision as to whether or not belief in God is reasonable. However, this would be quite different from regarding the existence of God as an empirical hypothesis akin to the hypotheses found in the typical sciences. In the latter, *particular* empirical experiments or observations become important, especially for the falsification of a hypothesis, often in a kind of "crucial" test. But metaphysical claims, including claims about the existence of a personal God, are not hypotheses of this kind. For what particular experiments or observations could possibly provide either verification or falsification of a scientific kind? It is true that in the history of Christianity some apologists have tried to use miracles in this way, but I have already argued (in chapter 2) that this is a mistake.

One might say — somewhat stretching the ordinary use of the word "hypothesis" — that human experience, taken *as a whole,* leads some people to support a religious hypothesis. However, not only do other people interpret experience differently, but this is quite unlike empirical testing by particular pieces of experience. Failure to see this is a failure to understand what a metaphysical claim is about. One might say, perfectly reasonably (and here I revert to my point that atheism can be rational), that one does not believe that the God "hypothesis" is coherent (which amounts to a version of logical positivism) or that one does not see the need for any metaphysical claim (which could lead one to atheism); but these positions are not the ones I am attacking as fallacious. To regard the

38. In fact, I am aware of some people who do pray in exactly this way.

God question as if it were really like a question in physics or chemistry is a mistake, and any argument based on such an assumption is fallacious.[39]

One of the complications within this issue is that some scientific hypotheses, notably within the field of cosmology, are concerned with the *whole* universe and not only with certain parts or aspects of it. It is interesting to note that for precisely this reason, a number of scientists are wary of such hypotheses, wondering whether or not there has been a merging of scientific and metaphysical questions. I do not know the answer to this, but I suggest that when cosmologists ask such questions, the kinds of tests or evidence that they are searching for are still empirical and not metaphysical, because they tend to rely on the observation of *particular* events or observations within the universe, such as "the red shift." There is still a search for some set of experiments or observations that could provide falsification of a hypothesis.

What I call a metaphysical hypothesis could easily be misunderstood. As I have already indicated, I am not denying that, in terms of the life stories of individuals, some people come to believe in God because of experience, either of a particular joyful encounter, or of what they consider to be an unexpected moment of grace. (A surprising number of people claim to have had a direct experience of the living Christ.[40])

39. In an article entitled "The God Hypothesis," in *New Scientist* (March 17, 2012, pp. 46-47), Victor Stenger makes a mistake similar to Dawkins's when he claims that God, or the gods, "if they exist, must have observable consequences." There is a sense in which this may be true, but not in the manner of providing empirically verifiable or falsifiable data. The error of treating religious claims as empirical hypotheses also emerges when he suggests that, if prayer were shown to be effective, it would imply, "scientifically," the reality of a god. This is questionable, since the skeptic would easily be able to find an alternative explanation, perhaps by combining Jung's theory of the collective unconscious with evidence for psychosomatic healing, and might well rule out, a priori, the possibility of a metaphysical rather than a scientific explanation. Once again, this indicates how different metaphysical claims are from scientific ones. Nevertheless, I have argued that metaphysical claims are open to a certain kind of rational investigation.

40. See Philip H. Wiebe, *Visions of Jesus* (Oxford: Oxford University Press, 1997). My reference to this book could easily be misunderstood. I am not suggesting that the accounts described prove the reality of God, or the resurrection, but that just as some people will naively accept such accounts as truthful without exploring possible naturalistic interpretations, so many materialists will simply rule out the possibility that something extraordinary may be going on because their worldview is being challenged. We are all

Equally, some people come to disbelieve in God because of a particular experience, perhaps one of bereavement. In such cases, however, it would be most unusual to claim that here was a kind of logical step of a kind that is any way similar to the verification or falsification of a scientific hypothesis. Sometimes no claim to a rational process would be made at all; in other cases — where a kind of rationality might be claimed — it would be more like saying that, as a result of a particular experience, one sees a new pattern in life *as a whole,* rather in the way that a collection of dots can suddenly seem to form a picture. In science, I repeat, the particular piece of evidence is crucial; in metaphysics, it is the way the whole is seen, though it may sometimes be true that particular events trigger this way of seeing or feeling.

The phenomenon of the "near-death" experience provides an interesting illustration of how a personal experience may cause a change in worldview. It is now established that a significant number of those who suffer cardiac arrest, and who seem to "die," recall after the event a similar pattern of extraordinary experiences, including that of going down a tunnel toward a light. One researcher in the field, the Dutch cardiologist Pim van Lommel, has found that 18 percent of those who survive recall such experiences.[41] I have personally known two people who have had such an experience. One, an atheist, was shaken by the experience but eventually concluded that it must have been physically caused, perhaps by low oxygen levels in the brain, and he remained an atheist (though a less dogmatic one). The other person was not only shaken but underwent a reshaping of his whole life, including a new affirmation of belief in God. Among the many things that cry out for further inquiry here is the claim that during these extraordinary experiences the brain is "flatlining" (i.e., there is no observable neurological activity).

My conclusion is that, while atheism itself is not necessarily irrational, the kind of atheism supported by Dawkins tends to be both irrational and dogmatic. Dawkins is right to insist that we should not believe

---

familiar with dogmatic religion, but people seem to realize less how often materialism can be equally dogmatic. Wiebe himself is eager to admit and to discuss the possibility of "neuropsychological" explanations of the phenomena he describes (pp. 193-211).

41. Pim van Lommel, *Consciusness Beyond Life: The Science of Near-Death Experiences* (London: Harper Collins, 2010; first published in Dutch, 2007).

things on mere authority rather than on the evidence; but he does not add that what counts as "evidence" depends on the context. In the hard sciences the evidence is essentially empirical, though even here there are aspects of science that are not purely empirical, such as when the human imagination generates fruitful and original hypotheses. In the human sciences, such as psychology and anthropology, the "evidence," though rooted in empirical observations, is even more clearly linked to theory; in the areas of human reflection, such as ethics and aesthetics, basic convictions, like the one that affords intrinsic dignity to persons, are not empirical in any ordinary sense of the term. This does not mean that there cannot be any "evidence" (e.g., about the sad consequences of not treating persons with dignity), but that what counts as evidence is not nearly as straightforward as in the traditional sciences. In metaphysics, and particularly in that branch of metaphysics that overlaps with theology, we have seen that evidence relates to how a "whole" is interpreted, rather than to particular aspects of the physical universe. An oversimplified account of evidence leads Dawkins to assume that all rational people will adopt something akin to his atheism, while I have concluded that perfectly rational people can be either theists or atheists, though not of the kind that caricatures the opposition — as is Dawkins's custom.

Relevant to the argument of this section is the suggestion (e.g., in the recent writings of Stephen Hawking) that new insights in physics make God unnecessary because the universe may have started as a spontaneous event, simply generated by the laws of physics. As several commentators have suggested, here is another confusion between scientific and metaphysical issues. The situation is rendered especially strange because, in order to explain the extraordinary suitability of the universe for the development of self-conscious human life, the suggestion about spontaneity is often coupled with the claim that this universe is one of many, perhaps of an infinite number of universes, ours being the only one, or one of few, that is suitable for the development of our species. I do not deny the possibility of other universes, but, in addition to the semantic problems concerning what we mean by a "universe," positing their existence is as problematic as positing a creative Mind as a source of this universe, and is arguably more in tension with the rationality expressed in Ockham's razor, or the "principle of economy."

It is important to note how ambiguous the term "materialism" is. In some contexts it refers to a kind of moral claim, namely, that the only ends we can properly pursue are "material" or egoistic. In this context, Karl Marx launched an attack on materialism in which he argues that our true nature is to be "species-beings" that should work for the whole of humanity rather than just the self. Elsewhere, "materialism" refers to the metaphysical claim that only matter exists, and in this sense Marx did indeed advocate a form of materialism. However, in this context it is interesting to note a series of subtle changes in what is meant by "matter." The stuff that atoms were once thought to be has more and more devolved into clouds of subatomic particles that often seem more like mathematical formulae than "things." Consequently, materialism has changed (some would say, retreated) from the belief in what most people understand as an underlying "substance" to something closer to Thomas Hobbes's view that everything can, in principle, be explained in terms of laws of motion. Personally, I fully support the scientific enterprise of trying to expand the role of scientific (lawlike) explanations as far as we can, but this is quite different from a kind of overall assumption, or even perhaps a metaphysical claim, that *everything* can be so explained. Here we might recall Thomas Nagel's claim that scientific reductionism cannot explain consciousness.[42]

The references to metaphysical claims call to mind the earlier discussion of how God, if he exists, must exist necessarily and not contingently. (Even though, as I have argued, the ontological argument is not valid *for us*.) The appreciation of this situation raises difficult questions concerning probabilistic arguments for the existence of God of the kind, for example, advanced by Richard Swinburne, because these, if valid, appear to show that God probably exists.[43] The problem is that in most cir-

---

42. Thomas Nagel, *Mind and Cosmos* (Oxford: Oxford University Press, 2012).

43. Richard Swinburne, *The Existence of God,* 2nd ed. (Oxford: Clarendon Press, 2004). Swinburne is aware of the issue, and he correctly contrasts "logical necessity" with the kind of "factual necessity" that God alone must have (p. 96). He concludes: "On our total evidence theism is more probable than not," and he sees his argumentation as a variety of inductive reasoning (p. 342). Although I hold that many of Swinburne's arguments carry weight (and though I also share his conviction that there are rational grounds for theism), I would make a stronger contrast between metaphysical arguments (for which probable percentages are not appropriate) and what we normally think of as induction.

cumstances the conclusion of a valid probabilistic argument would be something like: "There is a 50 percent chance that this fire was caused by arson." With inductive arguments there is sometimes a clear rationale why a particular percentage should be put on a probability, for example, on the chances of a horse winning a particular race, given previous performance and the running conditions. However, the "cause" of the universe is so unlike the alleged cause of a "thing" or of an event within the universe, like a fire or a race, that any analogy between the type of argument that could end up with a figure such as 50 percent and an argument designed to show that there is a Creator who exists necessarily seems very stretched. I admit that, from a strictly human perspective, a metaphysical argument may be more or less (psychologically) persuasive, and thus that we might regard some arguments as carrying weight or being "probable." But those arguments are very unlike the kinds of probabilistic arguments put forward regarding things within the universe, for which plausible percentages can often be given.

The description of "metaphysics" as (among other possible characteristics) an intellectual discipline that concerns "the whole" rather than the parts (as in typical cases of empirical, scientific arguments) invites a comment on the classical arguments for the existence of God. These arguments come in three main forms, and though most of the presentations can be strongly criticized, particularly in older forms such as those of William Paley, I believe that, properly stated, they still carry intellectual weight.

The kernel of the first (the "cosmological" argument) is that there is nothing intrinsically improper about asking the question, "Why is there something rather than nothing?" Once this question is granted as permissible, it invites the serious possibility that there might be an "answer" and that this answer points to a creative source that is then identified with the God of monotheistic traditions.[44] Rejections of the meaningfulness or significance of the question tend to depend on theories of mean-

---

44. Most theists believe that this argument provides for belief in a Creator ex nihilo. An interesting variation, known as "panentheism" (not to be confused with pantheism), is that the argument points to a kind of reality that transcends the physical universe, even though it is dependent on it, rather as (for Aristotle) any organism transcends the sum of its parts and thus has a "soul" of some kind.

ing or reference that can, in turn, be challenged. The kernel of the second (the "teleological") argument is that the particular nature of the universe, and its extraordinary capacity to bring forth human beings (along with their music), points to the possibility of a creative Mind, as in recent discussions of the "anthropic principle."

The kernel of the third (the "moral") argument, at least in one of its forms, is that we need some kind of creative Mind, which is also identified as Love, in order to make fully coherent the moral intuition that people (and perhaps animals) really matter, and that, for example, Kant's insight that we should treat all persons as ends in themselves, and not as mere means or commodities, is not simply wishful thinking. We may be conditioned to think in this way, but once we are aware of our own conditioning, our intellects cry out for some adequate grounding for those moral convictions that theists and secular humanists share.

E. The Doctrine of the Trinity

In the next section I propose to indicate the topics that liberal Christians are likely to explore when confronted with non-Christian religions, some of which have their own "liberal" variations. However, before reviewing these subjects, I want to provide a short discussion of the Christian doctrine of the Trinity, because it is perhaps the doctrine that, at least on the surface, is most clearly rejected by non-Christian religions. I will conclude by suggesting that, to a considerable extent, the doctrine is often rejected because it is misunderstood.

It is common to find the doctrine of the Trinity dismissed as "irrational" (especially by materialists and by non-Christian followers of monotheism), as something that is in conflict with any attempt to provide a "rational theology." I tend to prefer the term "liberal theology" to "rational theology," even though some writers speak of the two as virtually the same (e.g., John Tulloch).[45] My reason for this is that rational theology can too easily suggest an endeavor such as Kant's in his *Religion within*

---

45. John Tulloch, *Rational Theology and Christian Philosophy in England in the Seventeenth Century* (Edinburgh and London: Blackwood, 1872).

the Limits of Reason Alone, whereas I am seeking to give place to the possibility of treating human experience in the context of religion (or, more generally, the idea of revelation) as something to be taken seriously, a kind of datum on which rational reflection can work. However, it is also important to emphasize the role of reason within liberal theology, even with regard to doctrines such as that of the Trinity.

In the first chapter I emphasized the difference between the irrational (characterized by faulty argument or prejudice) and the nonrational (typified by a vivid personal experience, prior to any attempt to interpret it). As I have indicated, opponents of Christianity frequently describe the Christian doctrine of the Trinity as an example of the irrational, but I believe that this is a mistake. If the "one" in "God is one" were to refer to the *numeral* one — as within the sequence of positive integers (one, two, three, and so on) — there would be a strict contradiction with "God is three," and thus any doctrine of the Trinity would be an example of irrationality. However, in Christian theology this is not the case, because the statement "God is one" is much more like "this nation is one" or "I am one person," where "one" refers to an essential harmony rather than to an integer. Famously, Augustine compared the unity that makes up being a person (a harmony of understanding, memory, and will) with the unity that comprises God: that of Father (the creative source of all); the Son (the image, or *eikon,* of the Father, a kind of concrete manifestation of this creative source that is made available to us, in which we see the character of the eternal within a particular image); and the Spirit (a sense of divine energy within things, including ourselves).

I would argue that the Christian doctrine of the Trinity, properly understood, far from being irrational, is a blending of the nonrational with an element of rationality. The nonrational, which in the case of the doctrine of the Trinity is historically prior to the rational element, reflects powerful human experiences of (1) a sense of creative presence, especially when confronted with the wonders of nature; (2) the historical person of Jesus; and (3) an interior sense of energy that seems to radiate a divine power. The rational element arises from the attempt to provide some coherent account of a unity or harmony (or "oneness") that takes into account these diverse experiences. For example, just as understanding, memory, and will are not separable parts in Augustine, but essential "co-elements" in the unity that comprises a healthy human individual, so the persons of the Holy Trinity are not separable parts but essential co-elements (though this word, too, is inadequate) within any attempt to give an account of the divine — that is, as experienced by humanity.

It is totally consistent with this worldview to note an analogue to the doctrine of the Trinity in some non-Christian religions, where there has also been an experience of a divine reality. An interesting example occurs in Yann Martel's *Life of Pi*, where, within a version of Hinduism, there is seen to be a fundamental unity between the creative source of all things, signified by Brahman; the image of this creative source within the representations of Krishna, described by Martel as "Brahman made manifest to our limited senses"; and the internal energy that flows from this source within each person's spirit, described by Martel as "the spiritual source within us."[46] The chief difference between this and the Christian version of the Trinity is that, instead of a symbolic image (that is, not necessarily that of an actual historical person) such as Krishna, there is claimed to be an actual historical person, namely Jesus of Nazareth, who is the image, or the *Logos*, of God. Another difference is that Brahman is not usually thought of as a Creator ex nihilo. (I should point out that different versions of Hinduism use somewhat different kinds of "trinitarian" formulae, some of which are much less clearly analogous to Christian philosophy.)

In Islam, too, the issue is more complex than is often realized. God is one, but he has ninety-nine (or more) names, such as "The Just," "The Merciful," and so on. These names are "unified" or "harmonized" within God. (Sometimes these names are identified with the attributes of God, but some, including Al-Ghazali, distinguish between names and attributes.[47]) Again, the claim that "God is one" is not the end of the matter, but rather a beginning of the exploration of the kind of unity that makes up the Creator. Again, in all the great monotheistic religions, God is "transcendent" (sometimes described as the "wholly other") and yet is

46. Yann Martel, *Life of Pi* (Edinburgh: Canongate, 2002), chap. 16.

47. Al Ghazali makes a distinction between the attributes *(sifat)* and names *(ism)* of God, the former not being restricted to the latter. See his *The Ninety-Nine Names of God*, trans. D. B. Burrell and N. Daher (Cambridge: The Islamic Texts Society, 1992), pp. 177-79.

also "immanent" (because of the sense that God is also within us). Love can be understood as a kind of mediator between these two classical experiences of the divine, for it is love that flows from the creative source of all things, and for Christians, that leads the divine energy to enter our very beings and to enter human history in a unique way.

F. Some Typical Issues with Respect to
Other Religious Traditions

There are many religious traditions that offer alternatives to Christian liberal theology, and in some cases these alternatives are rational, in my view, in that they can be — and sometimes are — held by people of significant learning coupled with both intellectual integrity and high intelligence. These traditions would deserve extended treatment if this were a longer book. Some of these traditions are theistic, meaning that they include belief in what might be called one "personal" God (who is believed to be aware of, and to have relationships with, individual humans). These theistic religions include the four Abrahamic forms of theism (Judaism, Christianity, Islam, and Bahaism) and theistic traditions that do not stem from beliefs concerning Abraham and his covenant with God, including Zoroastrianism and Tenrikyo, as well as theistic versions of Hindusim and Buddhism.[48] Sikhism is a special case, being a form of personal theism that has links with the Abrahamic tradition through the influence of Islam.

Other religions are nontheistic in that they either deny or — more often — are not concerned with a personal God, even though some of them use the word "god" (meaning some kind of ultimate principle rather than a personal creator). These include Daoism, Confucianism, as well as many versions of Hinduism and Buddhism. Still others do not fit comfortably into either the theistic or nontheistic divisions. This applies, for example, to the religious traditions of a number of indigenous peo-

---

48. Tenrikyo is remarkable for a number of reasons. Its founder was a woman prophet (Nakayama Miki, ca. 1838), and in order to avoid the notion that God is male or female, Tenrikyo often refers to the Creator as "God the parent."

ples, some of whom worship a "Great Spirit," but also worship a number of more specific deities. It is not always clear whether these other deities are, as it were, special manifestations of the one Great Spirit (which would make it possible to say that there is a kind of monotheism implicit within the tradition), or whether they really are conceived as separate entities. Furthermore, this very distinction might be considered alien to their ways of thinking — that is, itself the projection of inappropriate, Western-style categories of thought.

Topics that liberal Christians are likely to explore when confronted with a religious tradition other than their own include the following:

(1) The search for common ground. In the case of all the major religions this is most likely to be found in (a) a belief in the priority of the "spiritual" life to a purely materialistic one; (b) some commonly valued virtues and principles, including various formulations of the golden rule.[49]

(2) In the case of those religions that use the term "god," or some equivalent, there will be a search for a more specific kind of common ground. This search needs to be sensitive to the fact that there are differences of emphasis even within the Christian tradition, for example, in the way God's sovereign will is related to his loving nature. In extreme cases, where "God," or a "god," is described in terms that cannot be reconciled with love and justice (as in the case of Moloch), then a Christian should hold that the term "God" is inappropriate. More often we face a more complex situation in which other people's beliefs do seem to be pointing toward the God whom Christians believe to be the loving Creator of the universe, but they seem to be describing the nature of God in a confused, or in some ways mistaken, way. For example, when I read aspects of Calvinist thought that portray a God whose decree determines, from all eternity, who shall burn everlastingly in hell, I have been tempted to say

---

49. The use of the word "spiritual" does not necessarily imply that human beings have a "soul," or "spirit," that can be separated from the body; but it does suggest that the human person is not adequately described in purely material terms. We are "persons" whose lives gain meaning through feeling, loving, creating, and thinking. Many atheists are quite prepared to speak of a spiritual dimension to life when it is described in this way.

that Calvin did not worship the same "God" that I do. However, I think this response is probably unhelpful and likely to show a lack of awareness of the historical contexts in which beliefs are expressed. Further, when I read Calvin's *Institutes,* I find that much of the time he is describing, very accurately, beliefs that I share with him. Therefore, I think it better to say that we are both seeking to worship the same God, but that, in my view, the presentation of God's nature in the liberal tradition is closer to the true one.

(3) The best-known world religions have large bodies of sacred writings, or scriptures, and those which do not have sacred writings do have unwritten stories or myths that are handed down orally. These sources are of great interest to all students of religion, partly because of the search for common characteristics and partly for the discovery of interesting differences among religious traditions.

It is important to ask at least two questions when we examine these sources. The first concerns whether the nature of inspiration is held to be verbal, or whether it is held to depend on a vision of a truth that is then expressed in human words. As we have seen, liberals have problems with the former view of inspiration — in any religious tradition. For example, though I find many inspiring passages in the Qur'an, I have great difficulty accepting that they are all *verbally* inspired, such as the command to sever the hands of thieves (5: 28) or the claim that Jesus did not really die on the cross (4: 156-57) or that a woman's witness — in matters concerning debt — should count for half of a man's (2: 282). As I noted in chapter 2, liberal versions of Islam are now emerging in which the doctrine of the verbal inspiration of the whole Qur'an is not seen to be essential for the faith, though it is not safe to express such views in some Islamic countries. As I also observed in the second chapter, this issue of the nature of inspiration must not be confused with the question "Is this source meant to be taken literally?" For example, one might hold that the creation stories in Genesis are verbally inspired, but that they are nevertheless parables, or poetry, rather than history. In other words, though there is no need to hold a doctrine of verbal inspiration, it is wrong to conclude that if one does so there is necessarily going to be a conflict with Darwinian theories of evolution.

(4) The nature and value of the individual person is described differently in some religious traditions than in others. This realization is important in the discussion of different traditions, not only because beliefs about the individual relate to fundamental questions concerning what we believe to be true but also because there are serious moral and political implications. If individuality and variety are ultimately unimportant, then it is more difficult to see why human rights and attempts to alleviate the conditions suffered by the poor matter as much as they do for someone who believes that individuality and variety are things to celebrate — indeed, that they are part of God's creative genius.

On this subject I must confess that I am more than a little mystified, because sometimes those who believe that the individual is of no ultimate significance show enormous compassion (witness the lives of many Buddhist saints within the *theravada* tradition), while very often those who profess belief in the intrinsic value of every distinct human being show scant regard for the poor and oppressed within their societies (witness the lives of many rich followers of Judaism, Christianity, and Islam). There is no doubt where Jesus stood on this issue: "Inasmuch as you did it not to one of the least of these, you did it not to me" (Matt. 25:45).

(5) All the major religions have associated with them what are sometimes called "mystical" traditions: these refer both to descriptions of the experience of some kind of unity with the divine (or with the universe or with one's innermost being) and descriptions of techniques in the life of prayer that assist one to realize such experiences. One of the most interesting things that emerges in the study of world religions is the discovery of certain common features of both these experiences in all of the religions. A Sufi mystic (usually within the Islamic tradition), a Hasidic Jew, and a Christian contemplative such as Teresa of Ávila seem, at least some of the time, to be speaking a common language.

For religious people this common language and experience suggests that there really is a spiritual reality that men and women of all the great religions are in touch with — and this explains the common ground. The secular humanist counters with arguments that (a) the similarities are exaggerated, and (b) insofar as the similarities exist, they can be accounted for in other ways, particularly by way of common features of human psychology and physiology, for example, the effects on the human brain of techniques that lower the oxygen level. Personally, I think that this is one of the places where there is a kind of empirical evidence for some kind of religious discovery (though not necessarily a Christian one) and that the humanist response looks rather like "special pleading."

Nevertheless, we must exercise care when we interpret the language of the mystics, and we must not be forced into either (a) claiming identities of experience when each account needs to be interpreted within the tradition from which it comes, or (b) suggesting, because of different cultural accounts, that there are fundamental differences when, in reality, the underlying experiences are the same. For example, it is common to find in both Hinduism and Buddhism the unitive experience expressed via the metaphor of a drop of water being absorbed into the ocean, which, for some, suggests a total loss of any individual personhood. However, we find exactly the same metaphor used by Teresa of Ávila: "Spiritual marriage is like rain falling from Heaven into a river or stream, becoming one and the same liquid, so that the river and the rain water cannot be divided; or it resembles a stream flowing into the ocean, which cannot afterwards be disunited from it."[50] However, as a Catholic Christian, Teresa certainly did not mean to imply that the individual human soul ceased to exist; rather, that the experience of unity is so great that this metaphor is a way of pointing to the experience. Metaphor is metaphor. My point here is not to deny the similarity of the experiences but to be aware of how different traditions interpret them.

(6) In addition to questions of fundamental belief and of moral practice, religious traditions vary enormously with respect to many other things, such as diet, codes of dress, and forms of worship. Here the typical liberal is likely to make a sharp distinction between things that are important and things that, though they are psychologically important because people feel strongly about them, are not issues about which we should attempt to get any uniformity. They reflect cultural differences that we should respect.

An example of a custom that should be universally condemned is

---

50. Teresa of Ávila, *The Interior Castle* (1577) (London: Fount, 1995), II, 5, p. 176.

what is sometimes misleadingly called "female circumcision" but is more accurately called "female genital mutilation." In fact, no major religion demands this practice, but it is widely found in some cultures, and it is sometimes given an importance akin to that of a religious tradition despite the terrible harm that the practice does to many girls and women. At the other extreme are questions of diet, where a huge variety of customs should properly be tolerated because they represent values within distinctive traditions.

The cultural role of some of these matters of custom (regarding diet or dress) is easily misunderstood. Take the case of the Jewish and Islamic prohibition of pork. Some people think that the origin of this custom was a matter of community health; others think that it has nothing to do with health (or that, in its origin, this was a secondary matter) because the early stages of many religions involve a system of taboos in which some animals are sacred and others are not. In either case, it is sometimes argued that in the modern world, when the alleged health concerns no longer apply or when the arbitrary nature of taboo systems is recognized, the dietary rule can simply be waived. But the issue is more complex. Cultures express and reinforce their identity and solidarity through a series of practices and actions that do not have to correspond to either a moral code or a health code. Provided that no harm is being done, the value of these practices should not be measured only by their conformity to logic or health or virtuous action, but in terms of their success in binding people together. Ritual action, fully entered into by a group of people, has a value for what it achieves in this context. For this reason — though, as a liberal Christian, I personally feel no need to refrain from eating pork — I do not consider the Jewish and Islamic custom of refraining from pork to be either irrational or silly.

However, in interfaith dialogue there are many issues that fall between customs that are obviously immoral (like female genital mutilation) and those that are in themselves morally indifferent, like many questions concerning diet.[51] One example is the ritual slaughter of ani-

---

51. Some questions of diet do raise moral issues, either because of the alleged effects on health or because they cause cruelty to animals. Mainstream vegetarians object to the eating of any meat or fish on principle. This is an issue I shall not pursue here, except to say that, though this position is not one I hold, it does seem to me to be perfectly

mals if they are not allowed to be stunned before being bled to death. (Some ritual slaughterers allow stunning, others do not.) It is often claimed that when animals are killed by having their throats cut, unconsciousness is virtually immediate because the blood supply to the brain is stopped. However, in the case of cattle, some of the blood supply comes through the vertebral artery, which is unlikely to be cut, so that — unless the animal has been stunned beforehand — unconsciousness is not immediate.

Another example concerns religious law that distinguishes between men and women in matters such as rights to marriage, divorce, procreative freedom, and so forth. I do not propose to discuss these issues here, but we may find that there are traditions within most of the world's great religions that can be called "liberal," in which a common mind on these matters is emerging. In other words, instead of being matters that divide one religion from another in a fundamental way, they may very often be matters that tend to divide more conservative from more liberal elements within each religious tradition.

---

reasonable provided health considerations, such as protein balance, are taken into account. Difficult questions only arise when vegetarians wish to impose their beliefs on others. (Among those who could not possibly change to a vegetarian diet without huge cultural loss — and very likely major health issues — are Inuit communities in the Arctic.) Quite different is the claim that many forms of meat and fish are obtained by methods that involve unnecessary cruelty, such as close confinement in the fattening of these animals and the modes of transportation. Here, in my view, there is a strong case for legal as well as moral sanctions.

Afterword

On looking back at this essay — which I have written over the past five years — there are three things that I feel should be added.

First, a further remark on "secularism": when this term is defined in terms of an overall philosophy in which there are no grounds for any religious commitment, or, more specifically, no grounds for belief in a personal God, then I have given reasons for why I believe that such a philosophy, though held by many sincere and intelligent people, is open to challenge — on both nonrational and rational grounds. However, when "secularism" refers to the conviction that the political order should be separate from religion (and, even more, from any kind of "theocracy"), I hold that liberal theology should support such "secularism." Indeed, I see it as an implication of Jesus' demand "Render unto Caesar the things that are Caesar's, and unto God the things that are God's." At the same time, it is perfectly possible for a secular state to have special regard for its cultural history (which might imply, for example, state support for the fabric of ancient ecclesiastical buildings, or an invitation to traditional religions to take part in major civil events); but the nature of both law and government ought to be essentially secular. India has succeeded in producing a secular state in the context of a Hindu culture, and Turkey, likewise, within an Islamic culture (in both cases, with certain reservations), and many Western democracies within variations on Christian culture. This is the way things should be.

Second, my defense of the idea of a Fall (when not seen as a historical event, and dissociated from belief in any original "guilt") can be further supported by contrasting this aspect of Christian teaching with that of classical Marxism. For Marx, human nastiness is the product of our environment, and especially, in its worst excesses, a product of capitalist materialism. He believed, therefore, that once a perfect society (or "true Communism") has been achieved, state and law can "wither away." In contrast, while I accept the idea that our environments can affect our natures for the worse, the idea that a perfect culture could naturally produce generation after generation of "morally good" people seems totally misguided to me. Each society — and every individual — can only achieve a significant level of virtue by a *process* that involves a struggle against egoistic elements within our psychological natures, natures that are the product of a long evolutionary process. Here, Aristotle (with his emphasis on *acquired* virtue) and Christian teaching have much in common. This is why I refer to the doctrine of the Fall as a "true myth" that has major implications for any adequate political philosophy.

Third, when I suggest (in chapter 4) that the Christian doctrine of the Trinity is a blend of the nonrational and the rational (in contrast to the "irrational"), I would like to address a remark to those many thoughtful people who regard Jesus as a good man, perhaps a perfect man, but no more. While I do not claim to be able to disprove views such as this, I suggest that they tend not to consider carefully enough Jesus' own teaching within his parables about the meaning of his coming. (In this context we might recall that Jesus' stories are the aspects of his life that are most likely to be remembered accurately.) In the parable of the vineyard (Mark 12), for example, he speaks of how the climax of Jewish history will come when the Lord of the vineyard, having sent a series of servants, decides to send "his only son." Now is the time of harvest, of the wedding, of the kingdom, of the challenge to respond to both the message and the person that Jesus represents. An appreciation of this teaching helps to ground the claim that Jesus represents a special kind of *eikon*, or image, that is compatible with some kind of Trinitarian thinking.

Index

Index

Intersexuality, 108
Irenaeus, St., 102
Isaac, 95-96
Isaiah, 121-22, 131
Islam/Muslims, 14, 34, 49, 83, 86, 89, 95, 102, 109, 139, 141, 150-51, 153-54

Jacob, 96
James (brother of Jesus), 102
Jeremiah, 38
Jerome, St., 39
Job, 25
John Paul II, 125
John the Baptist, 63
Jonah, 62-63
Jonson, Ben, 82
Joseph, 39, 53-54, 61
Joshua, 129
Judaism, 14, 25, 88, 114, 151, 154, 156
Judas, 47
Julian of Eclanum, 92
Jung, Carl G., 143n
Junia, 108
Justin Martyr, 35-36, 54n, 68-70, 88

Kant, I., 5, 17n, 25, 85, 103, 136, 148
Karma, 70
Karmi, Ghada, 95n
Kaufman, Gordon D., 107, 112, 131n
Kenny, Anthony, 10-12
Kenosis, 47
Kett, Francis, 78
Kierkegaard, S., 26, 30, 96, 130
Kingsley, Charles, 8
Krishna, 150

Langford, M. J., 23n, 26n, 43n, 50n, 65n, 84n, 110n, 111n, 113n, 120n, 138n, 140n
Latitudinarianism, 9, 86
Laud, Archbishop William, 89
Law, William, 34
Lazarus, 63
Leibniz, G. W., 49

Lenin, 49
Leo XIII, 21n, 101n
Lewes, John, 78n
Lightfoot, Joseph, 7, 99-103, 100n, 101n, 102n, 108
Lilley, Leslie A., 9n
Lindbeck, George A., 15, 29
Logical positivism, 2, 3n, 137n, 142
Luther/Lutheranism, 36n, 40, 50-51, 74, 77n, 108
Lying, 63

Machiavelli, Niccolo, 85
MacIntyre, Alasdair, 29
Magisterium, 118-25, 130
Mao Zedong, 20n
Marriage, 53-59, 56n, 57n, 80, 90, 123n, 134n, 157
Martel, Yann, 150
Marx, Karl/Marxism, 8, 20, 140, 146
Mary, Queen of Scots, 78
Mary, St., 14, 39-40, 53-54, 61, 65, 119
Mary Tudor, 79
Materialism, 3n, 104-5, 111, 113, 137-48, 152
Maurice, J. F. D., 8, 97-99, 103, 112
McGrath, Alister, 10
McGrath, Joanna, 10
Methodism, 8, 137
Meyendorff, John, 39n
Midgley, Mary, 112n
Miki, Nakayama, 151n
Milton, John, 28n
Minnesota study of twins reared apart, 54n
Miracles, 7, 48, 50, 59-66, 104-5, 119, 142
Mitchell, Basil, 107
Modernism, 9-10
Monism, 2, 137
Moral argument for the existence of God, 148
More, Henry, 68n
Moses, 25, 99n, 121, 122n

Index

Mullinger, J. B., 68n
Munificentissimus Deus (1950), 118
Music, 103, 111, 132, 139, 148
Mysticism, 30n, 154-55

Naaman, 116
Nagel, Thomas, 146
Natural law, 59n, 80, 126, 128, 133-34, 135n
Newman, John H., 4-5
Newton, Isaac, 73, 105
Nicaea, Second Council of, 121
Nicene Creed, 84

Ockham, William of, 145
Omnipotence, 43-44, 47, 71, 138-40
Omniscience, 43, 71
Ontological argument for the existence of God, 132, 146
Oriel school, 6n
Origen, vii, 7, 9, 14-15, 36, 70-71, 74, 76, 95, 98, 116, 127, 129
Orr, R. R., 35n
Orthodoxy/Orthodox churches, 33, 38n, 39-40, 53, 92-93, 119, 121

Pacifism, 94
Paley, William, 147
Pantheism/panentheism, 3n, 69, 147n
Pappe, Ilan, 130n
Parker, Archbishop, 101n
Pastor Aeternus (1870), 118
Paul, St., 38, 53, 56n, 57-58, 63, 93, 102n, 108-9, 133, 135, 136n
Pelagius/Pelagianism, 42-43, 92-93
Penington, Isaac, 94n
Penn, William, 91
Peter, St., 17n, 102-3
Pharisaism, 88, 120
Phoebe, 108
Pius XII, 52, 53n, 124
Plantinga, Alvin, 106
Plato, 17n, 23, 32, 46, 69, 121, 129, 131

Polanyi, M., 11n
Polkinghorne, John, 26, 47n
Pontifical Biblical Commission, 21n, 121
Poole, Eve, 112n
Popper, Karl, 30
Postliberalism, 15
Postmodernism, 15
Praestantia Scripturae (1907), 122
Prayer, 108n, 142, 143n, 154
Presbyterianism, 10, 80, 102
Prophecy, 47, 68, 89-90
Protestantism, 10, 13, 15, 17, 21, 32, 38, 50-52, 74
Providence, 27, 44-50, 60, 71, 104-5, 110
Providentissimus Deus (1893), 21n
Puritans/Puritanism, 53, 91
Pythagoras, 28

Quakers, 8, 92n, 93-94, 108, 139
Qur'an, 89, 95, 153

Rahab, 46
Raphael, D. D., 26n
Reason/rationality/irrationality, 1-2, 11-16, 20, 24-31, 46, 49, 55, 60, 62, 68-73, 80, 86-88, 96, 107n, 127, 137, 144, 148-49
Redemption, viii, 32-34, 52, 61, 63, 72-74, 116-17, 126, 136. *See also* Atonement
Reformation, 21, 75, 77n, 110
Reincarnation, 70
Rerum Novarum (1891), 123
Resurrection, 7, 32, 61, 63-66, 143n
Revelation, 7, 16n, 24-25, 29, 30-31, 73, 75, 89, 107, 129, 132, 149
Ritschl, Albrecht, 17
Roman Catholicism/Catholicism, 7, 9, 15, 17, 20-21, 32, 34, 38, 50-52, 80, 83-84, 114, 118-25

Sacra Virginitas (1954), 53n
Schleiermacher, Friedrich, 6n, 7, 13-17